The Quiet Storm:

A Celebration of Women in Sport

Alexandra Powe-Allred and Michelle Powe

A Division of Howard W. Sams & Company

Published by Masters Press
A Division of Howard W. Sams & Company
2647 Waterfront Pkwy. E. Drive, Indianapolis, IN 46214

Printed in the United States of America.

97 98 99 00 01 10 9 8 7 6 5 4 3 2 1

Library of Congress Cataloging-in-Publication Data

Powe-Allred, Alexandra.
The quiet storm: a celebration of women in sport / Alexandra Powe-Allred and Michelle Powe.
p. cm.
Includes bibliographical references.
ISBN 1-57028-186-6 (trade)
1. Women athletes -- United States -- Biography. I. Powe, Michelle. II. Title.

GV697.A1P59 1997 97-43293
796'.082'092273--dc21 CIP
[B]

Table of Contents

Credits:
Cover designer: Suzanne Lincoln
Cover photographer: Scott Cubberly of Cubberly Studios
Cover model: Elise Berry
Proofreader: Pat Brady

To Mom & Daddy
Thank you for always letting us dream.

To Robb
Thank you for supporting this dream.

Nancy Woodhull: A great woman who taught us that sometimes you fall down when learning to fly.

Thanks

Nancy Woodhull told us, "I think we're put on earth to make sure that everything carries on — and not that it fails when we are absent." Woodhull devoted her life to shattering the glass ceiling and to bringing along as many women as possible. A founding editor of *USA Today*, a former president of Gannett News Service, and senior vice president of the Freedom Forum, she was a trailblazer for women's rights and for improving perceptions about women in the media.

We were honored that she shared some of her wisdom with us, and saddened when she died in 1997 at the age of 52. But her work and her words do live on. And we thank her for her incredible influence and efforts in tearing down stereotypes and barriers.

We also want to thank all the athletes who lent their precious time to us. And special thanks go to the women who allowed us to call them again and again, bounce ideas off of them, and ask more questions. These great women never balked. They always graciously obliged. Thank you, Micki King, Dana Gelin, Robin Carr-Locke, Nancy

Woodhull, Lyn St. James, Tamara St. Germain, The Fabulous Sports Babe, Wendy Hilliard, and Clair Rheul. The staffs at the Women's Sports Foundation, Winter Sports Foundation, and the governing bodies of U.S. Swim Team, USA Gymnastics, and U.S. Track and Field, and all the other sports mentioned in the book promptly provided information in any way they could. Without these folks, contacting athletes would have been far more difficult, maybe impossible.

Without the support of Ruth and Peggy at Kindercare, many of our interviews and a great deal of the writing would have been impossible. Knowing that our babies were well taken care of helped us focus on this important mission.

Thank you, Greg Sun — the best friend of the women's bobsled team (and our favorite male bobsledder). And thank you, Joey Kilburn, for letting us dream (and slide). Thank you, Joe Millo and Patrick Scannell, for your undying support of the women's bobsled team. And a big thank you to David Roth for many hours of hand-holding, suggesting, editing, encouraging, boosting, and negotiating.

Most of all, we want to thank our parents for their undying support — tangible and intangible. Thank you, Mom and Daddy, for your love and the belief you instilled in us that we can succeed in whatever we do. Also, thank you for editing our book and paying our phone bills.

As we say throughout the book many times over: isn't cooperation such as this what sports are all about? Isn't this one of the great benefits of learning to work together? Together, our family and all the women and men who participated in this book have created something very special for anyone interested in women's athletics.

To all of them — especially our family — thank you for letting us be on your team!

The Quiet Storm:

A Celebration of Women in Sport

Introduction

From the beginning of this project, we were struck by the instant bond and camaraderie we felt with the women we interviewed. Initially, we were surprised by how much each woman opened up, talking for long periods of time. We wondered, didn't these women get to talk about sports or themselves very much? Didn't they have strong familial and filial support groups? But we soon realized that this open communication and cooperation were indicative of something much deeper, much more relevant than talking about sports. Every athlete conveyed a feeling of goodwill and trust toward fellow female athletes, a special bond between sportswomen. We came to realize that what we, the authors, have experienced as bobsledders is not isolated to our sport; rather our frustrations and joys, and the sisterhood that has developed between us, are representative of the experiences of female athletes generally.

More than just teammates, the girls and women who train and compete together share a very special, family-like relationship. U.S. Olympic basketball player Teresa Edwards, the only basketball player — male or female — to compete in four Olympics, sums it up well: "The joy of the party is just being with each other. It's a family atmosphere."[1]

An example of the relationship that develops is demonstrated by the following story. U.S. bobsledders Liz Parr-Smestad and Alexandra Powe-Allred were working as a team in Calgary in November 1995, alternating driving and braking for each other. The Calgary track descends a mountain through fourteen curves. During one trip down, before curve seven, the women's bobsled flipped over. Gravity dragged Alex out of the sled and onto the track, while Liz was able to slip under the front of the bob, forced to ride out the crash through every twist and turn of the track. What happened next left track workers and coaches laughing and all saying the same thing: men would never have done that.

When Alex stopped sliding and was able to stand again (and pull her pants up), she spied pieces of the sled in the track. Her mind raced. Where was Liz, and was she hurt? Alex began sprinting down the icy track without spikes, defying gravity and ice.

Meanwhile, Liz had been helped out of the capsized bobsled at the end of the run. Her first words were, "Where's Alex?" She was assured by first-aid officials that Alex was okay. In truth, a bobsled truck was following Alex down the mountain, unable to catch up with her. Nevermind that Liz had torn the ligaments from her sternum or that Alex had ice burns from sliding down the track. Witnesses reported that as Alex rounded finish curve and she and Liz saw each other, the two women ran toward one another, while everyone else listened to the track announcer's commentary on the public address system. *"She's coming around finish. . . . Smoooooth exit out of finish curve. . . . They've seen each other. . . . Now the other American woman is coming toward her brake. . . . They haaaave contact. It's a hug!"*

Beyond the strong sense of family among female athletes, there is also a sense of responsibility toward young female hopefuls, as demonstrated by the wide, enthusiastic response the authors received from so many celebrated athletes, coaches, sports commentators, entertainers, and businesswomen who credited sports for having given them the competitive skills needed to succeed in sports and business. These women were eager to tell their stories in order to extol the benefits of sports and to help inspire and raise the chances for success and happiness among today's girls and young women.

Olympic gold-medalist swimmer Janet Evans agreed to an interview because she believes in the importance of sports for females and wants "to give back to young kids.

"We didn't have books like this when I was younger," she says. "It's important to have female role models."

When Olympic basketball star Dawn Staley forced a bus driver to stop for a small girl who had been chasing the team for an autograph, she was demonstrating that sense of responsibility and inclusiveness. "You never know," says teammate Sheryl Swoopes, "it might change [that little girl's] life. We didn't have anybody to look up to — positive, female role models in sports. Now little girls can choose. . . ."[2] Indeed, little girls today can choose from an impressive pool of women to inspire them — women from all backgrounds, sports, professions.

The title *The Quiet Storm* was inspired by American powerlifter and bobsledder Krista Ford. We were discussing determination and adversity with her, and how women "fit in" to athletics. Ford told us that after powerlifting meets, most of the lifters would stay and socialize, but she was all business. She came to lift and was gone. Someone called her "the quiet storm," and it stuck.

It stuck with us as well. What title could be more fitting to describe the women in this book, women such as Julie Croteau, the first woman ever to play or coach college baseball? At age 17, Croteau sued her high school and the coach who denied her a spot on the varsity baseball team simply because "she was a girl." Now working for Major League Baseball, Croteau continues to knock down gender barriers, paving the way for young female athletes — like a storm.

There are currently some very good books on the market about the male-dominated culture in this country. One, *Reviving Ophelia* by Mary Pipher, discusses the "look-obsessed, media-saturated, girl-poisoning" culture we live in, and how this culture is harming adolescent girls. We were intrigued with the title of the opening chapter — "Saplings in the Storm."

Pipher notes that "Some women blossom and grow under the most hostile conditions while others wither after the smallest of storms," but wonders, "Under what conditions do most young women flower and bloom?"[3] We wondered why females *must* be flowers. Krista Ford, Dawn Staley, Julie Croteau, Bonnie Blair, and The Fabulous Sports Babe (just to name a few) are not "flowers." They are quiet, powerful storms, who remain capable, nonetheless, of *creating* flowers.

And create they have. As we talked to more and more athletes (of all levels) and businesswomen, we realized that these amazing pioneers have blazed trails, knocked down barriers that lay in their paths, blown apart stereotypes and images — producing a kind of rain and a life that grows after the storm is gone, bringing new hope to others.

Julie Croteau, who started as a "quiet storm" in high school, stormed on to play on her college team and to coach the men's team at the University of Massachusetts. She is now a television commentator on the game and worked on both the 1997 All-Star Game and the World Series.

That hope was illustrated recently during the 1996 Olympic Games in Atlanta, marked as "The Year of the Women." The women's basketball and softball teams (dubbed the "other dream teams" by the media), and the women's soccer and field hockey teams filled the stands, dazzling spectators with their athletic prowess, and entertaining and endearing viewers with group hugs, diving belly slides, victory dances, and cartwheels. Bob Hunter of *The Columbus Dispatch* put it this way: "When NBC finally got around to giving us more than a quick peek at the U.S. Olympic women's basketball team, we discovered why the network didn't put it on more often than it did. After all the hype NBC had given the men's Dream Team, it probably was embarrassed that the women played harder and with more emotion than the men, and that their games were a lot more exciting."[4] And Olympic host Bob Costas repeated with some humor a viewer's comment about the Centennial Games: "You mean there are men competing, too?"

Of course there are two sides to every coin. Reporter Cecil Harris observed: "There is no acceptable reason why women's soccer and women's softball didn't exist as Olympic sports until this year. Nor is there an acceptable reason why U.S. women still have few money-earning opportunities in sports after their Olympic experiences end. . . . If the International Olympic Committee truly cared about promoting women at the Games, it wouldn't sanction inclusion of the NBA's multi-millionaires."

Harris acknowledges that "things are improving, especially for U.S. women." But, he continues, "The Year of the Women at the Olympics? Not yet. That would require an almost equal number of male and female athletes with achievers of both genders praised for their efforts. . . . The Olympics have yet to reach that stage of maturity."[5]

We do have a way to go (women's bobsled, for example, has yet to be named an Olympic sport). But "the Year of the Women" still proved to be more exhilarating, providing more on-the-edge-of-your-seat excitement than any Olympics in recent memory. How many millions of us stayed up past midnight to watch the nail-biting conclusion of the women's gymnastics team finals? Male track athletes, football players, and our very own bobsledding brothers all admitted to being choked up by Kerri Strug's last vault. (In fact, at a Super Bowl bash, MVP Desmond Howard went looking for Strug and an autograph.)

Who will soon forget Strug, with a severely sprained and ligament-damaged left ankle, believing the team needed her score, racing toward the vault? Never before had the U.S. women's gymnastics team won a gold medal. While she ran down that ramp, millions of us were holding our breaths, crossing our fingers, and fighting back tears. When she raised her arms, we cheered and cried with her. The moment is etched in sports history, one of many great moments in the year of the women. There were incredible stories of perseverance and determination. Stories about mothers who trained around nap times to become the world's best, women who overcame physical disabilities to break world records. So when Kerri Strug raised her arms, wincing with pain, we could have sworn we heard her say, "There's more where that came from!" These women, like all the women we interviewed for this book, have made a distinctive mark on our world, creating sports history, and leaving us with memories that will burn in our minds forever. They have reached the rainbow after the storm.

For it is to the rainbow that we are drawn — the multi-colored rainbow of positives that results from women embracing sports, qualities such as inner-strength and self-sufficiency. *The Quiet Storm* tells girls and women of all ages and backgrounds how to embrace this strength — without having to lose their femininity or themselves.

Indeed, girls today benefit from the work of pioneers. So many battles have already been fought for them — fought and won. But there are still existing prejudices against females in sports, as in society, and a disproportionate number of girls drop out of sports by age 14. This is particularly tragic since these sports dropouts also drop out of high school more often, tend to abuse drugs and alcohol, and have more unwanted pregnancies than their sports-minded classmates.

One reason so many quit sports is negative pressure. As Donna Lopiano, executive director of the Women's Sports Foundation explains it, puberty is an especially difficult time for girls. "When [the adolescent girl] gets into puberty, when she cares more about what her friends think, she is extremely vulnerable. Another girl can come up to her and say, 'You may score 20 points, but I have more dates.' Or a boy could say, 'I don't like a girl who has muscles.'" And the pressure does not go away with adolescence. But the girl who is able to withstand the pressure is more likely to grow into a confident and successful woman.

Historically, women have been discouraged from being assertive, "especially in business where they don't want to be labeled the big bitch," says sports psychologist Shelley Shaffer.

"But once you've fought your way onto the playing field," Shaffer says, "you develop this sense of confidence and poise, that you have just as much right to be here as anyone else. And that carries over to the workplace, the community and social settings."[6]

The women interviewed in this book reflect that philosophy. They speak candidly about the challenges they have faced as female athletes and professionals, and how they've handled those challenges. They share stories — some funny, some sad, some inspirational — with which the reader can relate, stories which we hope will serve as a catharsis for the wounded female ego and a catalyst for continuing efforts toward progress.

Our subjects' experiences have tended to begin with difficult non-sports challenges that carry over into their athletic lives, then arrive at some pay-off. This book follows a similar pattern: what girls and women are up against when they choose to pursue athletics, how they overcome both non-sport and athletic challenges, and how they are rewarded. As becomes clear, the rewards are many and varied.

Along the way, we also discovered how much fun we are all having, and should be having — enjoying sports and each other and, in some cases, rediscovering ourselves. For us, the authors, perhaps one of the more enjoyable times in bobsledding is summer training camp. There are very few people in the training center, leaving us to ourselves. We are hard-working athletes and dedicated teammates but, shhhh, we're also having fun doing things we would have never done in high school or college for fear of what others might have thought of us.

Picture this: For three days powerlifter and bobsledder Krista Ford had complained she wanted a candy bar (something not provided in the training center's cafeteria). One of our teammates went into town and bought her a Butterfinger. After a hard day of pushing the dry-land sled, we dragged back to our room and found rock-solid, 185-pound Krista standing in our doorway, taunting us with her candy bar. "I've got a

Buuuuuutterfinger. I've got a Buuuutterfinger." As Alex walked by, she snatched it out of Krista's hand and tossed it to Michelle.

Suddenly, Michelle jumped onto her bed, tossing it over Krista's head to fellow driver Jill Bakken. Alex, Michelle, and Jill then proceeded to tease one of the most powerful women in the world with a Butterfinger — a Butterfinger she *really* wanted.

Another teammate, Chrissy Spiezio, joined the fun. She grabbed the candy bar and ran out of the room. Soaking wet, Chrissy might tip the scale at 130 pounds. But here she was, half-amused, half-terrified, running down the "do not run in the hallway" hallway of the Olympic Training Center with Krista thundering behind her. Like the women's Olympic basketball and volleyball teams who did each other's hair, or the Olympic swim team who got their nails done together, or veteran swimmer Janet Evans who did 14-year-old roommate Amanda Beard's laundry, here was a group of grown women truly enjoying each other's company, enjoying themselves — even acting like kids — and able to do so because of the unifying spirit of sports. That is what sports are all about: teamwork, camaraderie, friendship, confidence, and fun.

Let the reader beware! Because this is a women's sports book, there are female issues involved. Although we believe this book will benefit all who read it, there are bits of humor that are truly female.

For example, the women's basketball team at Cal-Berkeley was having a hard workout when everyone became aware of a maxi pad lying on the court. Everyone froze. Only the sound of a lone bouncing ball could be heard echoing off the gymnasium walls. As Trisha Stafford (now an ABL player) tells it: "We knew no one would claim it." But, suddenly, one of the team players broke from the pack, scooped it up, and ran to the locker room, leaving behind her the howls of her teammates, all rolling on the floor. Yeah, you probably had to be there, but for those women it was one of the funniest things they had ever seen. It is the kind of humor that perhaps only women can truly appreciate; but, in dealing with female athletes, we must deal with the issues of menstrual cycles, pregnancies, mood swings, and tampons that are part of us, too.

We do hope, however, that this book will appeal not only to women and to competitive athletes, but to men, recreational athletes, former athletes, and those who might have been but were not athletes. The message in the book is intended for athletes, coaches, parents, and fans. It is for women and for men. We believe that the experiences of the women about whom we have written show that everyone wins — male and female — when girls and women reach their full capabilities in sport and when they learn to reach their full potentials in life.

It is time to let the winds of female perseverance fell what they may and to let the rains of female progress water the seeds of the future. A rousing game of "keep the Butterfinger away from Krista" isn't a bad idea either.

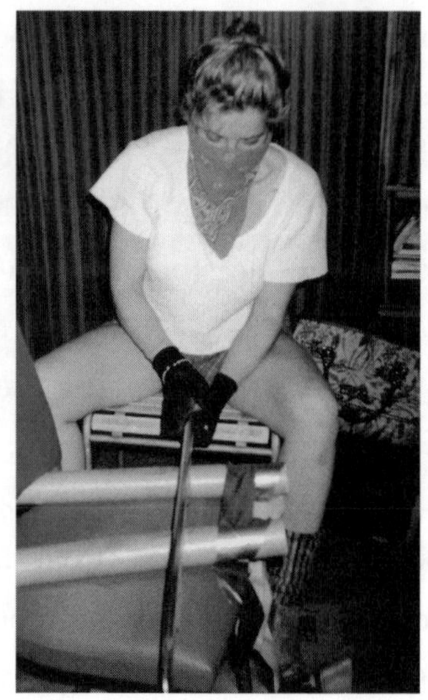

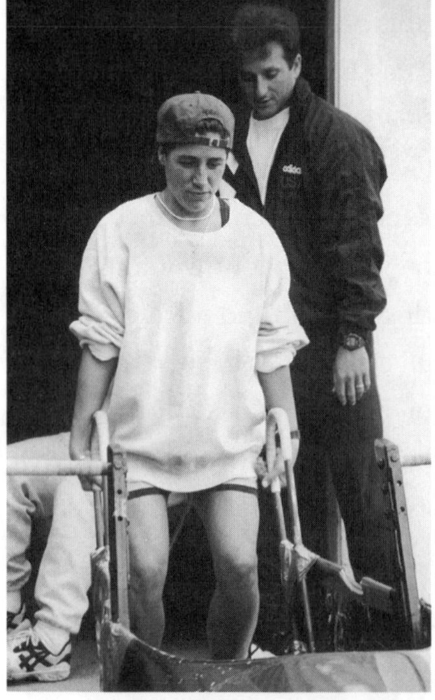

Scenes from the U.S. women's bobsledding team. On the left side,from top to bottom, author Alex and her driver Chrissy Spiezio in Calgary '96; team coach Steve Miarorca at OTC in Lake Placid watching over Chrissy Spiezio; and Krista Ford receiving help from a member of the Jamaican bobsled team. On the right side, author Michelle stays up late at night sanding her runners —a five-hour procedure.

Chapter One
Why am I Doing This?

> *Still the risk must be run; the mark made.*
> — Virginia Woolf, *To The Lighthouse*

We all have different reasons for selecting and sticking with (or not) our sports of choice and the accompanying hard work. For us, the authors, that hard work begins during Week One at Accelerate Ohio, training home of such sports stars as Chris Carter and Scottie Graham of the Minnesota Vikings, track Olympian and 400-meter world record holder Butch Reynolds, White Sox outfielder Rex Hudler, and Cincinnati Bengal Ki-Jana Carter. And now, it is also the training home of two members of the U.S. women's bobsled team.

Thirty-one-year-old mother of two, Alex, is running on the giant treadmill while 33-year-old Michelle is bent over at the waist, trying hard not to think about throwing up. Alex, however, can think of little else. After an hour of running at 12 miles per hour at a 30-degree incline, we are exhausted. But our trainer is telling us to pick up our knees. "High knees. High knees." In our weary minds, our knees are very high. The countdown has begun for how long we can last before one or both of us throw up.

This training program may sound like it is in direct contradiction to our assertions about having fun. In truth, we complain and we moan, but we love what we do! Almost all the athletes we interviewed said the main reason they got into their sport was "because it seemed like fun." There were some exceptions. For example, baseball player Croteau says she initially just wanted a high school varsity letter. Some athletes got into sports because an older brother said they couldn't. Some, like 6'5" basketball star Lisa Leslie, took up a sport because someone assigned it to them. "You should play basketball!" Some, like speedskater Pooch Harrington, even did it to meet boys. (To Pooch, Dutchie — skating around the frozen lake — was the cutest boy in the whole world.) Most, however, did it and continue to do it for fun.

The fun of sports, of course, is not limited to top athletes; all of the younger children we interviewed said they participate in sports for fun. While the parents may be signing kids up for exercise, social, and even babysitting purposes, the kids clearly believe fun and better health to be the reasons for joining a sport.

For whatever the reasons we participate competitively or recreationally, whether for weight loss or rehabilitation or Olympic gold or just to get away from the kids (or parents), we've probably all wondered at some point, "Why am I doing this? Why do I bother?" Perhaps, despite running 15 miles a week, the weight is not coming off. Perhaps, shin splints make every step painful. Perhaps, the kids have started tagging along. Whatever the reasons to start, and whatever the reasons to continue or to stop, they are sure to be of a personal nature.

But when these internal choices are reinforced by external pressure (such as sexual harassment or family discouragement), the resulting decision to quit or continue takes on much larger dimensions. Perhaps the kids are only tagging along because their father refuses to watch them. This is the usual sort of adversity women face. And females who try to participate in male-dominated sports face even greater-than-usual adversity. The young woman sprinting the stadium stairs in 90-degree heat for football practice may find herself, at the very least, the victim of verbal sexual abuse. ("This isn't a girl's sport.") She is questioned endlessly about her motives: Why are you doing this? Do you just want to rock the boat? And so she questions herself and the sanity of what she's doing. Is it worth all the criticism? Does *anyone* else think this is a good idea? Does anyone support her?

The same cannot be said of boys for whom participation and success in sports is not questioned. For females, however, resistance and self-doubt are normal. So why do some girls and women ride out the resistance and stick with their sports and convictions? There are as many reasons as there are female athletes.

Danielle Lundy

Eleven-year-old Danielle Lundy has been the national champion breaststroker in her age class for three years (1994-1996). She is trying to break into the record books as the first African-American breaststroker to make an Olympic team. Her goal is the 2000 Games. There is a lot riding on her small shoulders. Already, Lundy is approached by strangers who tell her they admire what she is doing, that they view her as a role model for African-American children and all kids striving for high goals.

Her father worries about these outside pressures. "It took me a long time to accept her goals," says father Roger Lundy, Jr. "Getting to the Olympics is an amazing feat on its own; to win a gold medal is phenomenal." But as Danielle's father began to study the national rankings, he realized what his daughter already knew: she has the drive, the passion, and the power to be the best. This is a little girl who has defied the limiting norm of "proper feminine behavior."

So, too, has U.S. powerlifter Carrie Boudreau. After being diagnosed with severe asthma and scoliosis, Carrie was told by her doctor that exercise would help strengthen her spine and her lungs. He probably did not have powerlifting in mind, yet she refused to let a medical condition slow her down. In fact, Boudreau — who "thrives on things stacked against" her — is the world record holder in her weight class and, according to *The Guinness Book of World Records*, the strongest woman in the world pound for pound. At 4'11", weighing in at 123 pounds, Carrie deadlifts 500 pounds.

Jackie Joyner-Kersee, also an asthmatic, knew at age nine that either athletics or the corner liquor store would run her life. Living in a crime-ridden neighborhood in East St. Louis with a liquor store on every corner, Joyner-Kersee made the local YMCA her safe-haven and never gave up her dream of being the best athlete she could be. When young Jackie told her teachers she wanted to go to UCLA on an athletic scholarship, she was told she couldn't — that her grades weren't good enough, that she didn't have enough money. Undaunted, Joyner-Kersee studied and trained harder than she ever had, and received a basketball scholarship to

UCLA (where she met track coach and future husband Bob Kersee). To those teachers who had not believed, Joyner-Kersee proved that anything is possible if you work hard enough. In 1994, she was named "The Best Female Athlete Ever" by *Sports Illustrated*.

Julie Croteau of Manassas, Virginia, also had a lot to prove to non-believers. The first woman to play men's college varsity baseball and later coach NCAA baseball, she was introduced to t-ball by her mother at the tender age of five. Mrs. Croteau had no visions of her daughter becoming a pioneer, but simply wanted little Julie out of her hair for the summer. But by age 17, Croteau had become an outstanding first basewoman — so outstanding, in fact, that the high school varsity baseball coach told her she was good enough to play varsity ball. But he also told her that she could not play because she was a girl.

This did not sit well with Croteau, whose parents had raised her to believe in herself, to be the best that she could be. So Croteau and her family sued the school for the right to play. While making national headlines, Croteau drew upon her family and a very close circle of friends for support. "We lost the suit," Croteau says. "At [age] 17, that was very hard to understand. The truth is, at first, all I wanted was that varsity letter." But it quickly became a challenge about principle. Like so many other female pioneers, Croteau started out quietly, letting the storm within her grow until she could not be contained. "At the time, I didn't even know the meaning of feminism."

The lawsuit, and subsequent ostracism at school, served as a hard lesson. Croteau had always believed she was equal to boys. It was difficult to discover that being better than most of the boys was not only not good enough, it wasn't acceptable. Doubly painful was hearing the coach at Osborn Park High School deny under oath that he had ever told Croteau she was good enough to play — especially in light of the fact that Croteau was invited to play semi-pro ball even before she went on to be the first woman to play on a men's collegiate baseball team (at St. Mary's College in Maryland). Still, the lesson was a hard one and Croteau was not the only one punished. To this day, Croteau believes that many of her good friends "ended their baseball careers and for one, the chance to be homecoming queen," by supporting her. "But even at 17, we knew it was the right thing."

Julie Croteau

A reporter covering the case thought so, too. As the co-owner of the Fredericksburg Giants, an all-male semi-pro baseball team in Fredericksburg, Virginia, he approached Croteau, offering her the chance for a try-out. She took it. "Earning a spot," Croteau says, "surprised a lot of people and vindicated me a little."

Never again did she question herself. During her five years with the Giants, she says she was treated like just another player. Then she played with the Silver Bullets, an all-female professional baseball team. Unlike other women who had to request a try-out, Croteau was recruited by the Bullets' coaching staff. A torn rotary cuff in the spring of 1994 led her to sports commentary for Liberty Sports. Then in that same year, she was offered a coaching position for the University of Massachussett's Division I baseball team. No woman had ever coached men's baseball before.

Again, Croteau found herself in the sports spotlight with people questioning her ability and motives. But this time she was not one of them. "What have I learned over the years?" Croteau asks. "To trust myself, be true to myself. People stared and there was some harassment," she acknowledges. "It was a hard job, but I reminded myself that men do this all the time. I could, too."

Such a radical idea — *If men can do this, I can, too* — has gotten plenty of us in trouble, but also has opened worlds of opportunities. The authors of this book got involved in bobsledding because people told us we couldn't, that it is not a sport for women. That drives us. We do it because we are determined to see women's bobsledding become an Olympic event. If not for us, then, for the young women and girls who follow us. Whatever reasons the athletes we interviewed had for getting into sports, all of the results were successful and the long-term benefits often phenomenal. The roads paved by all the pioneers mentioned in this book, by all pioneers everywhere, make life's journeys smoother for the girls and women who follow. And women who stick with their sports and convictions *are* pioneers. Every girl or woman who takes to the mound or tosses the old pigskin or pulls in a rebound is debunking stereotypes, breaking down barriers. In fact, every female who participates in any form of physical activity is special. As Olympic rhythmic gymnast Wendy Hilliard points out, all of us, "from tennis great Billie Jean King to a mall-walking grandmother, we're all accomplished. We're strong, healthy, competent, confident and empowered."[1]

When a girl or woman begins a new sport, any sport, she embarks upon that journey toward empowerment. She often must venture into unchartered territories, but when she succeeds she shows not only little boys that little girls can throw a ball as well as they, but she also shows little girls — proving to them that they can do anything, giving them the self-confidence to believe in themselves. And this is the ultimate reward.

It is why we work so hard. During Week One at Accelerate Ohio, we are pushing our bodies beyond any level we ever dreamed possible because we really want this. We want the thrills of the bobsled ride, and we want the respect of the other bobsledders. While trainer Steve Menapace screams, "high knees" at us and our thirty-something-year-old bodies respond with creaks and groans, 11-year-old Colleen Clark sits quietly waiting for her turn. Barely sweating, barely breathing, she is in this sprint training program because her brothers are. She does this because she thought it seemed like "fun."

Clark understands that there is often a double standard for male and female athletes — that females are not supposed to be tough *and* attractive. Yet she seems to have found the appropriate balance between who she is and what she wants. Yes, at the age of 11.

"I want to play sports *and* be a girlie-girl," she says with a wry smile. Her brother Greg, 13, teases her because she is always painting her nails and doing her hair. Still, she holds her own on the treadmill at 10 miles per hour and a 20-degree incline. "I can be feminine and a great athlete at the same time," says Colleen. When asked to name female role models, who did brother Greg choose? Colleen and Cindy Crawford.

Why Colleen?

"She's a straight 'A' student, she plays select soccer," he shrugs. "She's really dedicated; she's just really good."

Girlie-girl or tomboy, the question remains why do most of us do this? The name-calling and stereotyping of "manly" female athletes can be difficult to tolerate, particularly for young athletes. So we must rely on each other for support. And we must learn to recognize our own individual worths. As the flower says to Alice in the children's fantasy, *Alice in Wonderland*:

> "Just be, Alice. Being is sufficient. Being is All. The cheerful, sunny self you are missing will return, as it always does, but only being will bring it back."

In her book, Pipher (quoting Simone de Beauvoir) points out that adolescent girls too often "stop being and start seeming."[2] They bend to social pressures, putting away their independent selves, and adopting properly feminine personas.

This is why sports are so important. Sports give girls and women self-worth and confidence; they help them to be. We need to start helping more girls and women stay in sports, so that they may be strong and happy and become role models for girls who follow them.

And what about Cindy Crawford, one of Greg's two female role models? We talked with her trainer Radu Teodorescu, who confirmed Greg's belief that Crawford serves as a definite role model. Cindy Crawford? Really?

"Cindy became a person who explores," Radu says, "a do-er, an athlete." When Crawford first went to Radu, she needed to get in shape for a calendar. Nothing more. What happened next is very common in athletics. Crawford got an attitude. "She developed an immense self-confidence, a feeling of power."

As Crawford herself puts it, "The training transcended the physical. It taught me that I'm powerful — that I could conquer the world when I walked out of the gym."[3]

There is another edge to "why am I doing this?" Aa perverse as this may seem, it is the internal arguing: *"I can't do this! This is too hard."* that becomes so rewarding when we can finally say, *"I did it! I did it!"*

While Michelle and Alex run the treadmill, while Steve Menapace sternly urges us on, we complain, we stall. Oh, do we stall. But it's all part of the game. Stalling for time and arguing with trainers, as Radu tells us, is actually part of the initiation to his club. His clients, he says, have actually formed a kind of bootcamp club where they swap training stories. It's them against Radu, but for all their complaining, they love the training, and they love Radu. "Even as dedicated as Cindy is, sometimes she complains about [having to climb] the ropes." She's not alone.

Oprah Winfrey also has admitted to stalling with her trainer Bob Greene. "I'll decide to move furniture, hang a picture, take my time tying my shoes." Like Radu, Greene has humor about it. He knows the stall techniques — it is all part of the game. "We argue a lot about the procrastination factor."[4]

Why go on then? Why do this to ourselves? As both Greene and Radu can attest, the metamorphosis that has come over their clients says it all. "They are different people," Radu says. "Stronger, healthier, happier, more productive. Exercise becomes a component of preparing for everything else in your life."

At only 11 years of age, imagine how Colleen Clark is going to feel when she finishes her program, takes her speed test, and realizes what she can do! There'll be no stopping her!

Nancy Lieberman-Cline, former Olympian, current WNBA (Phoenix Mercury) player, and the first woman to be inducted in the Basketball Hall of Fame, believes so strongly in the importance of keeping girls in sports that she encourages communities to hold awards and grants banquets for their female athletes. "Three great things happen when those young athletes are honored," she says. "Girls and young women know their participation in sports is valued, encouraging the development of pride and confidence; people who learn of the sports achievements of girls and women are more likely to support them; and more girls will be encouraged to take part in sports."[5]

Encouraging the development of pride and confidence in females is so important. Nancy Woodhull, senior vice president of the Freedom Forum, co-founder of *USA Today*, and former president of Gannett News Services, had this advice for young females getting into sports today: "The important thing is to set realistic challenges and goals and work to realize those goals. Not every young soccer player will grow up to be a Mia Hamm. Not every young girl who dedicates herself to track and field will be Jackie Joyner-Kersee. If her goals are achievable, however, and she succeeds in reaching those goals, any young woman athlete has won something as important as a gold medal. The important part is realizing young women can succeed in a broad spectrum of activities and knowing what it takes to do it. You may not quite have the natural ability to be a star, but if you learn that discipline, conditioning and commitment will improve your game, no matter what level you are at or what game you compete in, you've gained valuable knowledge for the rest of your life."

Nancy Woodhull

Across the board, all the top high school female athletes we spoke to were on their honor roles. Becoming disciplined and committed in sport has clearly carried over into their everyday lives. For many, it is a quiet confidence. They know they can succeed in their sports. They know they can handle their studies. But when we asked many of the athletes about their grades, they would shyly say, "I do okay." Always the parent would pipe up, "She's an honor student."

Danielle Lundy told us, "Okay, I guess," in response to the question about her grades. Later, dad Roger Lundy, Jr., called us back: "I just thought you should know she's an honor student." He couldn't stand it; he had to tell us. But were we surprised? Not really. With these girls, there is no bravado about their school grades. It is almost as if they assume the good grades are part of the deal with athletics; there is no limit to what they can accomplish.

When Allie Sizler's parents were called into a parent/teacher conference with her second grade teacher, they were told "not to expect too much" of their daughter. Allie was labeled "slow" because of an undiagnosed hearing impairment. Now an honor roll student, the 15-year-old all-state basketball player is already receiving recruitment letters from colleges around the country. "The thing about Allie is she is an extremely dedicated and focused little kid," says father John Sizler. "She gives 150 percent effort in everything she does. At a very young age, she's very driven by athletics. That crosses over into her academics. Sports have really helped her with time management, and to keep her priorities in line."

She's not alone. Rachael Myllymaki turned professional in the Professional Rodeo Cowboy Association at the age of nine. *Nine!* She traveled the rodeo circuit; competed against some the strongest adult rodeo riders in the country; hauled trailers, horses, and equipment; and did her homework. She was an honor student all through school. And now a sophomore at the

University of Montana, with a full scholarship and still riding, Myllymaki has made a name for herself academically as well.

"I learned to just sit myself down and do what needed to be done," she says. Like mastering barrel racing, Myllymaki has also mastered her school work. She is an example of Lieberman-Cline's point that sports build confidence on all levels in girls and young women.

This point is particularly critical at a time when the rates of obesity in children and the incidences of anorexia and bulimia in teens are on the rise in this country. Girls who exercise are far more likely to have positive body images and healthy relationships, are 92 percent less likely to use drugs, and 80 percent less likely to have unwanted pregnancies. They are three times more likely to graduate from high school and, by exercising as little as two hours a week, have lower incidences of breast cancer later in life.

Pretty powerful plugs for sports.

The importance of young female athletes feeling significant and valued cannot be stressed enough. Particularly during adolescence, when so many girls are so unhappy and self-critical, imagine the glory of feeling special, needed, and important.

And benefits of physical activity certainly are not limited to young females. Menopause, the gradual change women experience from the reproductive to the non-reproductive years of life, can bring on many physiological changes. Hot flashes, fatigue, depression, weight gain, and irritability often are experienced. Osteoporosis and arteriosclerosis, changes which often occur later in life, can be devastating to a woman. The answer?

You've got it, whether in mid-life or later — exercise.

Cardiovascular exercise and weight maintenance can control mood swings and hot flashes, stimulate bones to retain the needed minerals to keep them strong and healthy, and reduce the risk of coronary artery disease through loss of abdominal fat, to name a few benefits.

At the age of 82, Mary Walker of Philadelphia still works full-time. During daylight saving hours, from April to October, Walker (how appropriate) walks seven miles home every day! In the morning, she takes the train to work and, unless it is raining, she walks home. She has done so for the past 25 years.

When told that during her career at the CoreStates Bank she has walked more than 25,000 miles, equivalent to more than an equatorial walk around the world, Walker was pleased. "That's incredible, isn't it?"

Yes, it is.

Walker is committed to her exercise program. "I just love it. Walking gives me a chance to meditate. It's good for the soul and quiets the mind. By the time I get home, all the little problems of the day have evaporated."[6]

Seventy-four-year-old Helen Klein of Rancho Cordova, California, has taken physical fitness to a higher plane, and is educating women about the benefits of exercise along the way. "There's too much separation between the mind and the body in our culture. What's the sense of living to 100 if you can't move?" An "endurance athlete extraordinaire," she receives weekly fan mail. And she is taken quite seriously by her far-younger competition. At the end of the 1995 Eco-Challenge, a 373-mile, 9-day race, a cameraman caught footage of a team that had passed Klein. "They were resting," Klein recalls, "when one of them looked up and saw me running down the hill. They were frantic. I heard one of them say, 'Oh my God! Here she comes! Get your packs! We gotta go!'"[7]

Klein, like so many of the athletes we talk about in this book, has bucked society's notion of "proper feminine behavior." Says the great-grandmother, "I was programmed to believe I'd be an old lady who couldn't walk a mile, who played bridge and went to lunches." Instead, she demonstrates to women that there is no limit to what they can do.

In some regards, physical activity is even more important as we get older — as women and as athletes. Most athletes believe that the talents of female athletes have not fully begun to be tapped until the late-twenties or early-thirties.

Trisha Stafford of the American Basketball League's San Jose Lasers basketball team told us, "I don't think women blossom as athletes until after our college years. No one ever sees that. As we get older, we are more in sync with our capabilities. Everything is in harmony."

When we repeated this to Gwen Torrence, she agreed wholeheartedly.

"Exactly! We, as women, get better with age. We learn more about our bodies and get more confident as we age. Men come into sports thinking they're God's gift. Women don't. We build up to it. Women in their late twenties and early thirties are the medal winners. Gold medal winners are always older. In track and field, our peak years are 26 to 33 years."

For this reason alone, Torrence advises young athletes to take their time in training. Torrence says she hates to see high school athletes pushing themselves too hard, and worse, coaches pushing unrealistic goals. "What kids don't realize is it's more than just running fast in a straight line. It takes time to mature." But, she warns, when they push and train too hard too soon, they burn out before their peak.

Her advice: enjoy yourself!

Beyond better health, better grades, and better relationships as reasons to join sports, there is another recurring theme: that special friendship, the bonding that female athletes share. Athletes have told us story after story about experiencing special "moments" with their teammates. During the Atlanta Games, swimmers Amanda Beard and Kristine Quance chased each other around their dorm with magic markers, coloring each other until they couldn't see their skin. *Sports Illustrated* reporter Alexander Wolff wrote of the women's basketball team: "In the Sunday's final, the American women parceled out 30 assists and mounted the medal stand holding hands, a gesture of togetherness that evidently hadn't crossed the minds of their male counterparts the night before. Gilt, you could say, by association."[8] In fact, reporter after reporter noted the closeness these women shared.

The U.S. women's soccer team was called "the team of sisters." And they were the team of aunts as well, sharing parental responsibilities for teammate Joy Fawcett's baby daughter.

Four-time Olympic champion speedskater Bonnie Blair confessed to us that perhaps more than anything else, she misses her teammates and the competitors from other countries who have become her friends over the years. "I've gone from seeing these people every day to occasionally having lunch with them. I really miss them." And U.S. luge veteran and four-time Olympian Cammy Myler confesses that after more than a decade of competitive sliding, she is going to deeply miss the friends she has made all over the world. They are her second family.

On April 30, 1993, during a break between sets, a deranged sports fan stunned the world when he stabbed super-star tennis player Monica Seles in the back. Although her wounds healed fairly quickly, the emotional scars of the attack kept her from competition for more than two years. As Seles tells it, "Night after night, I woke up in a sweat with my mother standing over me, frightened by my cries. I would ask her to sleep in my bed, to hold me like a baby."[9] Returning to tennis seemed terrifying to Seles. Slapping the ball back and forth with her brother, Zoltan, was one thing. To compete before thousands on an open court was something else.

Then, in February 1995, Martina Navratilova called Seles. Navratilova was flying to Florida for a tennis tournament and wondered if she could visit Seles. "Maybe we could hit a few balls for a while." They did.

Navratilova asked Seles to return to the game, assuring her that everyone missed her. And as she stood to leave, Navratilova unclasped a diamond tennis bracelet from her wrist, telling Seles she wanted her to have it. Seles protested.

"When you come back, you can return it to me," Navratilova told her warmly. It was just the kind of encouragement Seles needed. In July 1995, Seles played in an exhibition game in Atlantic City, N.J., against — who else? — Martina Navratilova.

Whether it was the bracelet or, more likely, the support of a fellow athlete that gave Seles the courage, she was back. Seles won the match, and as Navratilova hugged and congratulated her, she told Seles, "You're back, girl!" Seles happily gave back the bracelet.

There are so many pay-offs in sports — better health, strong bodies, strong minds, confidence, discipline, healthy relationships. And fellow bobsledder Courtney O'Neil told us about another pay-off.

At thirty-six, O'Neil had never been an elite athlete. In fact, she had had a lifetime of abusing her body. Drugs and alcohol had nearly ended her life on several occasions. Ruined relationships, financial woes, rocky employment records, DUIs and, subsequently, arrests played a much larger part of her life than she had planned. There seemed to be no controlling her own life while drugs and alcohol were involved.

In 1985, O'Neil woke up in a motel in Lake Placid, New York. She was in room number 0. She had received a DUI, had no car, and only a few fleeting memories of the night before. She had to ask her mother to drive from Connecticut to get her. That was the turning point in her life.

In 1995, she would return to Lake Placid to make the U.S. women's bobsled team, having been sober for ten years and in training. As each athlete met and discussed her workout regimen with Olympic weight trainer Jon Osbeck, O'Neil shared hers.

"What's your sport?" Osbeck asked. Most were soccer or track and field.

"Well," O'Neil smiled, "I smoked for eighteen years."

Later in the week, O'Neil traveled alone back to the fated motel. She found room number 0 and sat outside, watching the door for some time.

Look at me now, she thought as she returned to her room at the Olympic Training Center.

Talk about pay-off!

Chapter Two

Am I a Flower or a Storm?

The average preadolescent girl is oblivious to negative societal messages; she is busy climbing trees, challenging boys to arm-wrestling matches, and usually winning. She challenges boys verbally as well. She is happy and confident and assertive.

> *Over the fence —*
> *Strawberries — grow —*
> *I could climb — if I tried, I know —*
> *Berries are nice!*
> *But — if I stained my Apron —*
> *God would certainly scold!*
> *Oh, dear — I guess if He were a Boy —*
> *He'd — climb — if He could!*
>
> —Emily Dickinson

So what happens? Why, so often, does that assertive child grow into a passive adolescent? In a brief span of time, as she crosses the line separating preadolescence and adolescence, childhood and womanhood, that young girl completely changes her demeanor. Gone is the tough-talking, tree-climbing tomboy; enter the "prom queen."

Schools play a major role in promoting this prom queen image of the quiet and pretty girl. A 1992 study conducted by the American Association of University Women (AAUW), entitled

"How Schools Shortchange Girls," showed that boys are twice as likely to be viewed as role models, five times more likely to be called on by the teacher, and twelve times more likely to speak up in class than girls. Classroom material is slanted to appeal to boys rather than girls, having three times as many boy-oriented stories. The study also found that boys are given more detailed instruction by their teachers and praised for academic work, while girls are praised for appearance and behavior.

And the bias is not only gender-focused; it has racial overtones as well. While studies have shown black girls to be more assertive in the classroom and to have better self-images than white girls, they are seen as boisterous and unruly for speaking out, and — as a result — are ignored more by teachers. In a study of first graders, black girls were praised for social maturity, while white girls were praised for academic success. When compared with white boys, the black girls were praised for their accomplishments, while the white boys were reprimanded for not reaching their full potential. The subtle message to black girls and white girls alike: don't bother trying any harder to excel academically because you have limited potential, unlike boys for whom the sky is the limit. While white boys still receive more positive reinforcement than black or hispanic boys, boys on the whole receive more encouragement than girls.

The statistics tell us discrimination is a very real problem, but *somebody* forgot to tell that to Jenna Brader.

It is Week Two at Accelerate, and Alex and Michelle are dying. Both the speed and incline of the treadmill have increased. The intensity level of the workouts is actually scaring us. While we huddle near the water fountain, wondering why the trainers are trying to kill us, 11-year-old Jenna stands by the treadmill, daring them to make her workout too hard. It isn't that they won't try, it's just that Jenna knows they're never going to break her.

"Who is that?" we ask.

Jenna Brader

We are told her name and that she is an all-state basketball player.

Basketball?

Jenna stands four feet six inches. She can't weigh more than 70 pounds.

She may be small, but basketball and speaking out have never been problems for Jenna. She fits the typical female jock profile: honor student, healthy, articulate, confident. So confident, in fact, that at one point during an interview we asked her mother if she was sure Jenna is only 11. Jenna's not afraid to speak out in class or shine on the court.

"I wish you could see her when she plays," her older brother, Joshua, says of Jenna. When she plays three-on-three, Jenna is up against girls twice her size and she gets the ball almost every time. "I'll take her to the 'Y' to play, and she'll start dribbling the ball, passing it between her legs. She'll be all decked out in her Nike stuff, the wrist bands and everything. Grown men will stop and watch her play. She'll be shooting three-pointers and guys will come up to me and say, 'Is *that* your sister?'"

She looks like a little doll: creamy skin that only a Campbell soup kid could have, big brown puppy eyes, a perfect little nose. But on the court, she is — as her brother describes her — "an animal." "Jenna," he says with understatement, "is real aggressive."

Not much intimidates Jenna. Not even adolescence. She understands that this is a time of physical change. And many girls do have trouble during this time. For just as their bodies are beginning to metamorphose, hips rounding, fat-cells increasing and breasts developing, girls are bombarded with the media female image. Rail-thin models and actresses with big breasts push anything and everything from potato chips to toilet cleaners. It is impossible for any female to escape this self-image sabotage. Girls focus on what is everywhere before them: the perfect female image. Perfect body. Perfect face. Perfect hair. Perfect clothes. Adolescent girls fixate on material things and obsess about their bodies. While boys in puberty think, "I'm getting strong," girls think, "I'm getting fat."

And feeling fat, especially in comparison to their male peers, is very often understandable. Dr. Wayne Westcott, fitness consultant and researcher for the YMCA, conducted a body composition analysis on second-, fifth-, eighth-, and eleventh-grade students in the Hanover, Massachusetts, public schools. Of 630 students studied, the average percentage of body fat for boys in all four grades was below the recommended level for males (15 percent). The girls' average percent of body fat increased from 21 percent in grade two to 24 percent in grade eleven.[1] While Westcott explains this as a normal pubertal change in female body composition, girls still think, "I'm fat."

So it's easy to see why so many girls give up on sports. It's pretty tough to muster up storm power when one is obsessed and mortified about changing body parts. It is a confusing time.

This book's authors serve as examples of the confusing flower-versus-storm images. While a pre-adolescent Michelle wore exclusively mini-dresses (it was the 70's, afterall) and ran with limp wrists, the younger Alexandra was the terror of the neighborhood. While Michelle collected butterflies and dog statues and constantly fussed with her hair, Alex played war and saved her stitches (acquired from jumping off low buildings) so she could throw them in her sister's hair.

Our flower and storm roles were set at an early age. But, then, a strange thing happened. While Michelle was a late bloomer (devastating by prom queen standards), Alex developed early (devastating by tomboy standards).

Every night Alex would beat her chest, hoping this would stunt her breasts' growth. And she would stand on her desk chair and jump off, landing on her bottom on the floor in the hope of keeping her hips from changing. Her thinking was it *really* hurt to do that, so surely it had to stop the growth process. While Michelle (along with millions of other girls) was performing her ritualistic "I must, I must, I must increase my bust" exercise, Alex was beating her chest like Tarzan gone wild. For her, development was robbing her of her storm power. In fact, development became so devastating that Alex actually dropped out of sports because she was embarrassed about the size of her breasts. She was so embarrassed by comments boys made when she ran that she stopped running altogether and began playing with her hair and make-up.

For Michelle, developing late was equally devastating. She endured insulting comments by neighborhood boys about her undeveloped physique every day of the eighth and ninth grades. The damage to her self-esteem took years to undo. But she began playing sports and, slowly over the years, became a storm. Eventually Alex, too, re-attained storm status.

Anyone who remembers suffering through adolescence is sympathetic to the low-esteem of so many teenagers today. Becoming a storm, or holding onto that storm power, is a state of mind. It means mastering your emotions rather than letting your emotions master you. It is believing in yourself, loving yourself, and knowing you are worth all things. But these are not common feelings among adolescents whose self-images are generally at an all-time low.

Tia Trent is an example of how important good self-image can be. An all-state high school track star, Trent had an undefeated record her sophomore year and set school records in the 200, 400 and 4x400 meter relay. During her speed test at Accelerate Ohio, Trent was clocked running 20 miles per hour. She maintains a 3.0 grade point average while running track and playing basketball. But these are not her greatest feats. Trent's self-confidence and sense of determination are so strong, they are almost startling in one so young. Before our interview with Trent, her coach Irv Christenson (who once coached Olympian Bob Kennedy) warned us, "Tia does what Tia wants." He was right. Raised by a mother who constantly told her that "you're the greatest" and to "think big," Trent knows who she is and what she wants to accomplish. Although she has a brother who plays professional basketball, Trent is her own person. She has refused to take any money from him for college; she plans to earn a scholarship on her own merit.

Tia Trent

How does she rise above peer pressure about how she should behave? Simple. She ignores it. She redefines femininity to fit her. She recognizes that her future doesn't depend on boys; it depends on her, and her willingness to work hard. So Trent's stand on boyfriends also is simple. She doesn't have time for them right now. She is serious only about her school and sports. These, she says, are the things that are going to take her places. "Boys don't know what they want," she explains. "At this age, I don't know if he's gonna graduate. I don't need to get weighed down by all that and a baby." While she understands that may happen to some of her classmates or friends, Trent has vowed it won't happen to her. "If a guy has his head on straight, he'll be comin' to *my* meets." And any boyfriend of Tia Trent's should know what he's in for: a smart, athletic, attractive, strong-willed young woman who has every intention of making sports history. "I'm looking to make history for my own name and title."

Also looking to make sports history is Karla Keck, ranked second in the world in Nordic ski jumping for women, with her eye on the world record. Keck also has overcome tremendous pressure to quit (no coach, no training facilities, no sponsors). She has done so because she knows she is good and knows she is right. And she loves what she does. She has been jumping for 16 years, since she was five years old. She was always one of the best, beating the boys. "I lost of couple of my best friends [male] after I beat them," she says.

When she turned 18, the guys were all looking to the Olympics, and she was supposed to go away. (Nordic ski jumping and bobsledding are the only two winter sports that do not yet include women in the Olympics.) But Keck has no intention of going away, despite lack of funding and support. She is determined not only to participate in the Olympics as a nordic ski jumper, but also to win a medal. In fact, she is training in Norway to try out for the U.S. men's 1998 Olympic team. (She made the junior Olympic team, winning the trials, in 1991.) The confidence she has acquired from her athletic successes far outweighs any social pressures to the contrary. And Keck's determination and energy have grown as she has, unfolding as a quiet, but mighty storm. She is a pioneer in her sport, dedicated to her own pursuit of excellence, but also to paving the way for other females in future Olympics.

Participation in athletics, however, is certainly not the only way to further the cause of female sports. Tamara St. Germain's own dreams of Olympic glory in skiing ended abruptly with a broken femur in 1992. Despite her personal loss, she still wanted to be able to give back to women's sports some of what she felt she had gained. She wanted to encourage young girls to give themselves a chance. Appalled by the amount of drug and alcohol use by local teenage girls in Lake Placid, New York (site of the Olympic Training Center for winter sports), and by the fact that "nearly half of the high school's senior girls were pregnant," St. Germain resolved to do something. She founded the Winter Sports Foundation (formerly the Winter Sports for Girls), now based in Boulder, Colorado, a non-profit organization that introduces inner-city kids to the world of sports. "Being able to share what I love to do most and seeing the expressions and reactions of the girls [have been] the most rewarding experiences of my whole life," she says. St. Germain stresses that girls need athletic role models, just as they need academic or professional role models. They need the confidence and self-esteem to know that they can do whatever they choose to do.

Scenes from the Winter Sports Foundation. Top two photos on the left: Tamara St. Germain works with inner-city kids in Boulder, Colorado. On the right: Girls can even learn to bobsled at the foundation's headquarters! Bottom: Tamara and some of the other teachers at the foundation relax -- the woman on the far right is Karla Keck.

This is difficult, however, when we are still inadvertently teaching girls what their limitations are. Wouldn't it be nice if we could pass out flyers on young women like Rachael Myllymaki or Danielle Lundy?

Too few teachers and parents are challenging girls as much as boys. One teacher, however, who does challenge girls is Greg Williams, a fifth grade math teacher in an inner-city Columbus, Ohio, school. Williams believes education, exercise, and self-esteem are all interconnected. And he has created the concept of "mathercise" to further that notion, combining mathematics and exercise.

Fitness, Williams says, has always been presented in a negative sense. In boot camp, soldiers are ordered to "drop and do 20" push ups for disciplinary reasons. "I switched that," Williams laughs. When one of his kids answers a math question correctly on the board, Williams booms, "Right! Now, give me 15 push-ups." Kids, he claims, love the challenge. Learning and exercise become fun. More importantly, at this age, his female students see that not only can they do the push-ups (and math), but many times they can do more push-ups than the boys.

A little girl approached Williams after class one day. "Not athletic at all," he remembers, she confided in him that she had been doing exercises at home. "She was very smart, but never believed in herself." It was no surprise to Williams, then, that as the girl became more physically fit, she also became more confident and more vocal in school.

"Catching that fourth or fifth grader at that age and instilling in [him or her] the importance of health, self-esteem, and fitness is so important. They can think, 'Okay, not only am I capable, but I can do things — all kinds of things.'"

I can do all kinds of things. If men can do this, I can, too. This is what we need to be teaching girls. And sports are a means to that end.

Sports allow girls to act out, speak up, become notable through their actions, giving them the confidence to be assertive. Sports give them more positive self-images, stronger self-esteems, and allow them to focus on internal rather than external characteristics. Sports teach them teamwork and the ability to be competitive on (and off) the field/court, but still walk away as friends.

As beach volleyball star Gabrielle Reece says, sports force girls "to work as a team with other girls, to work together under every possible condition — winning, losing, tired, grumpy, happy. It forces them to deal with unpleasant, ungracious emotions and get over it. It forces girls to rely on each other. It gives them confidence in other girls,"[2] which ultimately gives them confidence in themselves.

But self-confidence is still one of the biggest problems for girls. It plays a role in how they approach everything they do and in how they perform. Girls, for example, apologize far more than boys, saying sorry if they miss shots or bump into other players. During our sprint training regimen at Accelerate Ohio, one of the trainers told us she preferred girls on the treadmill over boys any time. "Girls are so easy," says Shanda Eickelberger. "They do whatever you tell them. The guys always complain, try to argue their way out. On the whole the girls work harder. Because they have been told by people they can't do something, they have something more to prove."

Other trainers also have told us they think the females are more prone to put forth a greater effort because they have something to prove. But they also concede that lack of self-esteem and confidence play a key role in the performance of females, something we saw demonstrated at Accelerate Ohio. For many girls, the intensity of the training program is new to them, and so is handling the stress and fatigue. "Most girls don't play sports or really get into something until they're in fifth to sixth grade," trainer Mike Neff says. "By that time guys are already trying to touch the top of the door frame. They're always testing everything." Girls don't question their program on the treadmill because most girls aren't experienced in testing their boundaries. It is socially ingrained in us to stay within the established bounds. When we step outside, we are labeled. So, very often, we stay safely inside and our self-confidence diminishes.

"The entire time I've been here," Neff laughs, "I've never seen a girl try to touch that exit sign," pointing to the fingerprint-smeared exit sign hanging ten feet above the ground. It is a challenge too tempting to resist for the boys.

But Coach Pat Diulus laughs at the thought of Sameka Randall passing up such a challenge. Randall is the Associated Press' 1996 Ms. Basketball and a member of the 1996 Junior National Team. "Are you kidding me?" Diulus asks. "No doorway is safe from Sameka. I'm always yelling at her for hitting the basketball rim. She's not that tall (5'10"), but she has incredible jumping power. I'm afraid she's going to hurt her hand on the rim one of these days, but I can't stop her." The temptation is too strong for her to resist.

Randall is unusual. When her mother urged her to play with Barbie dolls, Randall chose the basketball court. While her mother was worried she would get hurt, Randall looked for pick-up games with the guys. The rougher, the better. Either someone forgot to tell Randall the "rules" about little girls, or she wasn't listening.

Sports teach kids that kind of confidence and self-esteem — the ability to see their own inner beauty and worth, to believe in themselves. And sports teach girls how to set and obtain goals, how to deal with defeat and go on — learning from these experiences and becoming stronger because of them. As Cammy Myler puts it, "In sports you acquire abilities applicable to anything: goal-setting, determination, perseverance, all the potential to make you a winner that carries over to everyday life."

And Myler's winning ways are, indeed, carrying over into her everyday life. A world-class luger, Myler is also an accomplished artist. The U.S. Luge Association has an "adopt-an-athlete" program through which Duofold, a long-underwear manufacturer, has sponsored Myler. With the help of her sponsor, Myler presented her first show of twelve oil pastel/abstract paintings in 1996 at the New York Athletic Club. With a successful showing under her belt and the paintings sold, Myler now has turned her efforts to law school and continuing to train for the 1998 Olympic Games. Through competitive sports, Myler has developed goal-setting skills and determination. Nothing can stop her now.

Ironman athlete Julie Moss says that the strength — physical and emotional — acquired through sports is particularly important for women. "You have physical strength, but you also have inner strength to attack the other things you want to do in your life," she says. "When women become empowered physically, it helps them to become empowered in all other aspects of their life."

Sports, in short, teach girls how to be part of and succeed in society, and the world of work. After all, says Tamara St. Germain, goal-setting and strategizing are the very characteristics necessary to succeed in the business world. "That's what business is.

Ninety-nine percent of women never get the chance to feel these benefits, which is why men run most businesses."

In *Games Mother Never Taught You*, Betty Lehan Harragan argues that to become a "player" in the business world, one must learn sports terminology. Learning about game plans and strategies (not to mention coaches and officials) is the key to success, because games (traditionally male games) are the training ground, the preparation for life and business. As children we understand that some kids can run faster than others, throw better, or jump higher. As teenagers, we understand that it is nothing personal when the coach puts in the better players; but we also know in many instances we can control our own fate by lots of practice and dedication. Playing team sports teaches us about human nature and relationships, general on-the-job rules.

Harragan says in real life, in the business world, women tend to cling to the notion of fair play and take turns, while men apply their "football" rules and forge ahead.

Freedom Forum's Nancy Woodhull, also the executive director of the Freedom Forum's Media Studies Center, agreed with the sports analogy. "The experience of dealing with adversity, defining solutions, and believing in their ability to achieve," Woodhull said, "is an advantage men [have] brought to the business world for decades.

"My advice to young women entering the business world is plan to succeed. By that I don't mean you should figure out how to become CEO before you even leave the personnel office. I do mean that, like the athlete, you should set achievable goals and then be willing to do what it takes to reach them. Realize that only you can really define success, and it won't always be at the top of that mythical pyramid. Set goals you can reach — like sports. [When you reach those goals,] set new ones, if that's really what you want. Don't allow society to set you goals. Make your life *YOUR LIFE*."

The benefits of participation in sports speak for themselves, some of which we've already mentioned: girls who do learn sports/life skills have stronger family relations, are better connected to their parents, have better self body-images, do better in school, and stay away from drugs and alcohol more than non-active girls. They also do better in business, learning networking and essential skills that foster success with organizations. As Wendy Hilliard says, "It's no accident that 80 percent of the female executives at Fortune 500 companies characterize themselves as having been 'tomboys' in their early years."[3]

First Lady Hillary Rodham Clinton's father used to throw footballs to her in the front yard; her mother played tennis with her. And both parents cooked. As Clinton explains it in her book, *It Takes A Village*: "Children learn what they see. When they see their fathers cooking dinner or changing the baby's diaper, they'll grow up knowing that care-giving is a human trait, rather than a female one. When they see their mothers changing tires or changing fuses, they'll accept troubleshooting as a human quality, rather than a male one."[4]

Women such as Robin Roberts of ESPN, Pam Oliver of Fox News, Christine Brennan, author of *The Cutting Edge*, and radio talk show sensation Nanci "The Fabulous Sports Babe" Donnellan have transformed the competitive and goal-setting skills they learned on the playing field or from their love of sports into a springboard for success in their professions. Their determination is summed up by Oliver, who worked first as a news reporter, and for eight years did sports reporting on her own

Christine Brennan

time and dime. She volunteered for non-glamorous, unpaid assignments until she finally earned the attention and respect of ESPN Sports. Says Oliver, "I wouldn't accept that my dream of being a sports broadcaster was *not* going to happen."

Brennan, who was a sports reporter with *The Washington Post* for several years, also never doubted her plan to become a sports writer, to write about what she loved. "From the time I can remember, I was out in the backyard throwing the football with my dad. That was something I wanted to do. Every day I listened to the games on the radio, watched double-headers. If I could have the perfect day, I would play sports all day long. That would be my perfect day."

Brennan is a storm in her own right. She was the first full-time female sports reporter at *The Toledo Blade* and *The Miami Herald*. She acted as the first president of the Association for Women in Sports Media (AWSM) from 1988 to 1990 and has covered the Olympics since the 1984 Los Angeles Games. Like Tia

Trent, flower power never occurred to or appealed to Brennan.

These women each learned that women have the right and the ability to be in the board room and in the locker room. They managed to rise above societal pressure and focus on their abilities, to view themselves as talented and effective, and they did so with far fewer female role models than kids have today.

Role models are critical. That's one reason the new American Basketball League (ABL) and the Women's National Basketball Association (WNBA) are so important. U.S. female basketball players have been playing in Europe for years, making well over $200,000 a year. But now many of these athletes have decided to stay home to play the game here, taking salary cuts of more than half in some cases, because as both LaShawn Brown and Sonja Tate of the ABL's Columbus Quest told us: someone has to make the sacrifices. Someone has to show this country's kids that women can be athletes, role models, leaders — anything they want to be. Both Brown and Tate feel very strongly about showing little girls they do in fact have something to dream about. And San Jose Laser Sheri Sam, known as an aggressive, sometimes trash-talking player, agrees: "Someone had to give up something, so we did. Now, all the players are committed to the league (ABL); we're taking chances."

Why?

"For the little kids who watch us," Sam explains.

So little girls can dream. And it seemed appropriate that the majority of the players for the San Jose Lasers and the Columbus Quest, during recent practice sessions, wore t-shirts that read: Little Girls Dream.

Given the sense of family and the dedication to fans we saw with the U.S. Women's Olympic Basketball team, we suspect the

ABL and WNBA will retain the same sense of community and leadership. Little girls can dream.

All the little girls who write to Oliver, Brennan, and the Sports Babe, or hang out after games waiting for an autograph from the ABL or WNBA players, wishing to be like them, now see that their dreams are attainable. When Oliver gets letters from little girls saying they want to be the next Pam Oliver, she still says to herself, "Huh? You can do better than that." Her point is that girls should see no limits today. Just keep trying, never give up, and dreams can and will come true. Keep knocking down walls and breaking down barriers. Be a storm that breeches the barriers and helps to carve out the path to real equality of opportunity in athletics and in life.

Go find the strongest woman in the world and tease her with a Butterfinger!

Chapter Three
The Goddess Within

The Year of the Women certainly had an impact on young girls everywhere. Everywhere there were reminders of women's Olympic successes – magazine covers with smiling female medalists, television interviews, best-selling autobiographies. Young girls began signing up in droves for gymnastics, swimming, track and field, basketball, soccer, softball. Our girls had caught the fever. But the year of the women also was gratifying for older athletes. As we watched women from all sports, women of all shapes and sizes, all skin and eye and hair colors, all different kinds of backgrounds win the hearts of Americans and the world, there was a certain feeling of coming into our own.

> *"I have failed once again to fulfill the expectations of others, which have become my own.*
>
> *I used to think of my body as an instrument, of pleasure, or a means of transportation, or an implement for the accomplishment of my will. I could use it to run, push buttons of one sort or another, make things happen. There were limits, but my body was nevertheless lithe, single, solid, one with me.*
>
> *Now the flesh arranges itself differently."*
>
> — Margaret Atwood, ***The Handmaid's Tale***

Most importantly, we finally saw that it is time to rechannel the anger and let go of the insecurities. While writing this book, the authors were repeatedly asked by male interviewees: "Is this a male-bashing book?" Anger was assumed. And certainly women have been held down long enough to have cause for anger. But anger no longer serves us. We've proven time and time again what we are capable of. Now we must remain focused and positive.

Still, as far as we have come, the persistent power of this beauty thing has us at a loss — even now.

Everywhere we feel its pressing influence. Marathon runner Patty Driscoll, for example, was preparing for the Boston Marathon in the mountains of Vermont. Alone with her thoughts, pushing herself along the isolated highway, she suddenly found that she had company. An 18-wheeler barrelled down behind her. She edged over, making room. The driver leaned out and shouted "Wide load!"

"Oh, yeah?" she shouted back. "Up yours, asshole!"

The truck disappeared around the bend of the mountain, but not before Driscoll made sure the driver saw — in his side-view mirror — her obscene hand gesture. Then, as she came around the corner, she saw the driver had pulled his truck over to the side of the road. Panicked, she slowed her pace.

Is he going to kill me? Beat me? I shouldn't have yelled that at him. I shouldn't have flipped him off. Now, he's mad.

Cautiously, she neared him, still unsure of what she should do. He climbed out of the cab and said, "Ma'am, I yelled 'wide load' because I was coming by with a wide truck and didn't want you to get hurt." He tipped his baseball cap, crawled back into the cab, and drove away.

It was a long run home, Driscoll says, especially since she felt only three inches tall. The anger from past hurts had kept her from focusing on the tangible and the positive in the present.

Another, more well-known marathoner, Joan Benoit Samuelson, was so embarrassed about her abilities when she first began running that she would stop and pretend to look at flowers every time a car passed. She went on to become the first woman to win Olympic gold in the marathon in the 1984 Olympics, but she had to struggle to overcome her insecurities about others' perceptions of her as an athlete and as a woman.

Indeed, a problem for women in sports is that females are judged by harsher standards of appearance than are males. Even the world's best female distance swimmer fell victim to the harmful scrutiny so often applied to girls and women. During the 1988 Seoul Olympics, a 17-year-old, 90-pound Janet Evans took the pool by storm, earning three gold medals. When next we saw her during the 1996 Atlanta Olympics, Janet was no longer a girl, but a young woman, two inches taller and 20 pounds heavier.

"Wow," people said, "look at Janet. She's ballooned." But she had not. She had become a woman. Now, there were hips, more rounded thighs, a bust line. Her body mass had changed from waiflike to slim. Evans says she had to stop reading newspapers because of all the references to her size. "The media," she says, "can develop. . . your image of yourself."

The harsh expectation that a waiflike body is the ideal still exists, particularly for young females. But the real pressure exists mostly within ourselves. The top athletes we interviewed all were comfortable with their bodies, quietly confident. While they work at their sports to become the best, they discover and rediscover themselves. They know exactly who they are. They know exactly what they are capable of. They know and appreciate their bodies. They know that strong is beautiful.

Case-in-point: a teammate recently visited Alex's house and saw a picture of her with longer hair standing next to the Mediterranean Sea. The teammate said, "Alex, you look like a downhill skier!" Ah, the ultimate compliment for an athlete. To be compared not to a model or movie star, but to another powerful athlete.

As gold medalist swimmer Angel Martino says: "A muscular woman is a beautiful woman. It was hard for me in high school. There were a lot of guys who wouldn't go out with me because I was too muscular. I think muscles are beautiful. . . . If I have a little girl, I hope I will be able to make her feel like being an athlete is beautiful."

But for young girls only beginning sports, or not involved in sports at all, thinking of a strong muscular female body as beautiful may be a foreign concept. As they gain weight during puberty (typically 35 pounds), female adolescents are continually bombarded with airbrushed images of "emaciated models and actresses with breast implants." Weight — or rather, weightlessness — has become equated with beauty in our society. "Society's standard of beauty is an image that is literally just short of starvation for most women." In fact, since 1979, "Miss America contestants have become so skinny that the majority are now at least 15 percent below recommended body weight for their height."[1] The average height and weight of a model is 5'9", 110 pounds. The height and weight of the average American woman: 5'4", 142 pounds. According to Hollywood director Joel Schumacher: "Sophia Loren and Marilyn Monroe could not get a job today. Their agents would tell them, 'Go on a diet, get a trainer.'"

Karen Rothmann, an elementary school teacher for 18 years in Washburn, North Dakota, has seen the perception of body image change over the years she has taught. Many of her students are very insecure because their self-worth is wrapped up in their bodies. "They want to be stick-thin, they want to be beautiful, they want to be popular, and they want a boyfriend," she says. These are their priorities. "For a lot of my little girls," she says, "that's what beautiful is — stick-thin."

Rothmann told us about one of her students who had stopped eating lunch. Melanie would go all day without eating. When Rothmann questioned her about it, Melanie said "the only thing she could control was her weight. She was trying to keep up with her older sisters, to measure up to them." By the spring, Melanie had lost so much weight that she was having to belt her pants to keep them up. Rothmann spoke with Melanie's mother, noting the significant weight loss, but was told not to worry about the little girl. Her mother said that she was very proud of the nine-year-old for using self-control.

Jenni Huelsman, a successful long distance runner at age 17, initially tried her hand at softball, but spent much of her time on the bench. She felt frustrated by her feelings of helplessness and worthlessness, by the way she was treated by her coaches and teammates. She became anorexic because, she said, weight was the one thing she could control. Eventually, she turned to running and it was running that gave her back control of her life. "I wanted to feel stronger and feel better about myself," she says.

She saw sport as a way to define herself. As a softball pitcher she felt unimportant to her teammates and coaches. As a runner she found her niche. Ranked fourth at her high school, Huelsman has proven to be a strong, consistent runner. "How do I define myself?" she asks proudly. "I am a runner. I know what my body can achieve. I know what I can do and I'm proud of myself!"

Sports allow, even encourage, that process of self-discovery, of learning who you are and what you can do. As Rothmann puts it: "It is so important for girls to develop so they know what they can do and feel good about their bodies. But I don't see that happening."

While boys are busily judging their female classmates on a point system, girls are desperately trying to measure up to the "standard." And they put pressure on one another to conform to this unrealistic and unfair picture of "femininity," making those in sports more reluctant than ever to strip down to athletic shorts, to "act like boys," and to risk social criticism or ostracism.

In fact, few teenage girls discover their true bodies. A staggering 75 percent of them diet rather than exercise, but even more disturbing, younger girls are dieting, too. According to some studies, as many as 50 percent of nine-year-olds have dieted, and 80 percent of ten-year-olds already do not like their bodies. Reported cases of anorexia and bulimia have doubled since 1970. But cases of obesity are up as well because kids do not exercise. Dr. Wayne Westcott, who is on the President's Council on Physical Fitness and Sports, says, "In the last fifteen years we've seen 50 percent of children fit into the obese category. There has been a 100 percent increase in super-obesity with these kids. It's very sad."

Exercise guru Tony Little told us what, we thought, had become a common place these days — you must have exercise as part of any diet plan. And, in fact, he does not like the term "dieting" at all.

"When you diet for a period of time, lose the desired weight and then stop, what happens? Eventually, most people go back to their original eating habits and gain the weight back. It's what starts the yo-yo dieting." Little maintains that if young people learn the importance of exercise, healthy eating habits happen more easily and better self-esteem and self-worth result. But yo-yo dieting and obesity in our children are sure to continue as long as adults don't value physical education, he says, because they don't pass that value onto kids.

So it came as no great surprise to us when we interviewed a group of kids in our neighborhood that there was not a serious athlete among them. We had witnessed chain smoking, alcohol abuse, teen pregnancy, truancy, and school drop-outs among these kids. We had heard about girlfriend abuse. We asked the teenagers about their perception of beauty, diet, and self-esteem.

We sat on the front lawn of Alissa's house with her circle of friends and her mother and sister Ashley, and we talked about role models. The group never concluded who good female athletes were, but they agreed that actress Julia Roberts was a good role model. Only Samantha named her mother (prompting Ashley to look at her mother and say, "Sorry, mom." She hadn't thought of that one). And Alissa and Ashley's mother, Marty, chose Hillary Clinton as her role model.

The boys had an even harder time than the girls identifying female athletes. They determined that aerobics, golf, swimming, and gymnastics were the sports that fit the picture of "proper feminine behavior." Sports that had been "made easier for girls, like softball" were acceptable. Male-dominated sports, such as bodybuilding, were not. In fact, female bodybuilding, in their opinions, was "disgusting." Brent did suggest that mud wrestling for women was acceptable. And breasts came up a lot.

The issue of breasts is one that continues to plague female

athletes. All of the female athletes we talked to about body image — young and old, recreational and Olympics — agreed that media images of Playboy bunnies and Hooters' servers do not make the road to athletics any easier. Even more damaging than the message that breasts are the essence of a woman is the cross message that breasts are a sign of weakness, an inconvenience, or just plain offensive. Take, for example, the incredible remark by sports commentator Ben Wright during the 1995 LPGA tour that women will never be great golfers because their breasts get in the way. And then, there is the example of *Oneworld*, a magazine that "celebrates diversity and encourages free expression," a magazine forced by its printers to place two black bars over the full breasts of one model in a full-frontal nudity photograph, but which allowed Asian model Zhing to bare all. When questioned about this contradiction, a spokesperson for the magazine said of Zhing that "her breasts weren't big enough to be offensive."[2]

While the boys were discussing breasts and Pamela Anderson Lee of "Baywatch," Danielle was still trying to come up with a good female athlete role model. Eventually, she chose Kim Zmeskal because she could do "flips and stuff." But Danielle conceded, "Female athletes don't get enough attention." So true.

In fact, *Sports Illustrated* writer Dana Gelin reported to us that in the magazine's questionnaire for Olympic athletes, even the majority of female athletes named males as their "most admired athlete." Three members of the U.S. women's basketball team chose Jackie Joyner-Kersee and the rest named men: Carl Lewis, David Robinson, and Michael Jordan. (In fact, 15 percent of all the 500 U.S. athletes who responded to the poll named Michael Jordan.) The U.S. synchronized swimming team named Dan

Jansen, Mark Henderson, Dennis Rodman, and Mary Lou Retton.

Surprisingly, the U.S. women's gymnastics team *all* said Michael Jordan, except Amy Chow, who answered Mary Lou Retton. The majority of track and field and soccer athletes also named male athletes. Gwen Torrence of the U.S. track team said Michael Jordan, and Chris Weber and Mia Hamm of the U.S. soccer team named Wayne Gretsky and Jackie Joyner-Kersee.

Wendy Hilliard

When Wendy Hilliard, president of the Women's Sports Foundation, speaks nationwide to schoolgirls, she asks them about their role models. And, like us, she's always disappointed with the answers.

"I always ask them who their favorite sports persons are," Hilliard says. "They name Michael Jordan or Shaquille O'Neil. I say, 'Ladies, we have a problem here.'"

A problem, indeed.

Hilliard's concern is a legitimate one. If girls and boys only see male sports figures, they are exposed to only part of the sports world. Specifically, they are exposed only to a world which seems to exclude females.

But we would have expected female *athletes* to recognize each other more. Of the girls we interviewed, more than 90 percent of them named female athletes. (Many of them also named Michael Jordan.) Did they know we were writing a book about female athletes? Yes, but ever the optimists, we like to think this had no bearing. Jackie Joyner-Kersee, overwhelmingly, was the name most given by younger participants in our interviews. Most girls also named female athletes in their same sport, and since there are far fewer female professional athletes than male, this would explain male athletes being named so much. For women basketball players, for example, players at the highest level of their same sport would have to be men's professional basketball players, since until 1996 there were no professional women's teams.

However slowly the wheels of progress may seem to be turning in the area of gender equity, they are surely turning. Women's sporting events are drawing ever-increasing numbers of fans and more women athletes are seen doing product endorsements. And major publishers are finally getting into the game, launching sports magazines for women. *Sports Illustrated* launched a spinoff magazine, *Sports Illustrated Women/Sport*, in Spring 1997 for women athletes and fans, and is planning a TV sports show aimed at women. Conde Nast Publications (*Vogue, Glamour, Self,* and *Allure*) introduced *Conde Nast Sports For Women* in Fall 1997. And *Jump*, a health and fitness magazine for teenage girls (published by Weider Publication, Inc.), also premiered in September/October 1997.

But even with all these changes, we are still caught in a time warp, limited by prejudices of the past. There has been a changing of the guard as more and more women enter the sporting arena — whether as athletes or as commentators — and body images become more positive and realistic. But the Old Guard — of male television executives and sports executives — still stands in many arenas, protecting its boys-only clubs. The Old Guard still believes women inferior, unable to perform the same tasks as men on the playing field, blaming female body parts.

The Old Guard still resolutely clings to the notion that viewers prefer men's events (in tennis, for example), and therefore justifies pay inequities between the sexes. But there is a new "Old Guard" in town. Not the conservative, status-quo protectors, but us — the Thirty and Up Club of female athletes. And this new Old Guard does its best to protect the Jenna Braders and the Colleen Clarks of the world, making sure that they focus on sport, focus on positive rather than negative, believing that they too can turn pro because — after all — Dawn Staley of the Olympic Women's Basketball team is only five feet, six inches tall, and Holly McPeak of the Women's Professional Volleyball Association is only five feet, seven inches. So while the Jennas and Colleens of the athletic world do their thing, we do ours — pushing for change and trying to topple the antiquated "Old Guard."

But those old boys are still pretty firmly entrenched and resisting progress, though we are chipping away. Part of that old "Old Guard" institution is the ever-popular *Sports Illustrated* swimsuit edition. While the debates continue on whether "cheesecake" belongs in a sports magazine, Clark offers this thought: "Maybe it would be okay if they took out the people and just showed the suits." Colleen's mother laughs, saying, "I don't think that's what they're after, honey." In 1997, though, for the first time, *Sports Illustrated* included actual athletes in the swimsuit edition. It is a start. We're doing our stomach crunches in case they call next year.

Steadily, females are moving toward better self-image and confidence as sports play a bigger role in young girls' lives. Muscle is in. Trent told us that one day, as she was walking down the street, a schoolmate told her, "Girl, you got good lookin' legs. Comin' up behind you look fine. But in front, you got no chest."

"I said," Trent reports, "'Okay, my family isn't breeding for big breasts!'. . . Like I'm gonna be able to sprint with big boobs."

Enter Florence Griffith Joyner. Known to the world as Flo Jo, she crashed onto the world scene at the 1988 Seoul Games. Like no other female athlete before her, she wore one-legged spandex running pants, and her long, painted nails glittered. She wore make-up and had long hair which flowed behind her as she blazed down the track. She was beautiful and flamboyant. And it was a package that everyone bought into. Her family didn't breed for large breasts, either. But what the Griffith family did produce was a woman who could run 23.5 miles per hour in the 100 meter. They produced a woman who broke track records in the 100 and 200 meters that still stand today, and they produced a woman who stresses again and again that "believing in yourself" is the key to all things.

But it is still difficult for young females to ignore the negative images, the prejudicial preference for physical attractiveness that is everywhere. A *Sports Illustrated* article about figure skater Katerina Witt described her this way: "She's so fresh-faced, so blue-eyed, so ruby-lipped, so 12-car pile up gorgeous, 5 feet 5 inches and 114 pounds of peacekeeping missile."[3] More female pictorials are dedicated to the swimsuit issue in *Sports Illustrated* than to female athletes. And every month the cover of *Muscle & Fitness Magazine* features an extremely muscular man with a noticeably non-muscular bikini-clad woman draped over him. (The May 1997 cover actually featured a female body-builder. Unfortunately, the editors still couldn't help themselves and had a non-muscular bikini-clad woman standing slightly in front of the athlete.)

Such classification of female athletes by their physical attributes rather than athletic abilities discredits all female athletes.

We are not seen as powerful, strong, determined, competent, but as sexy, graceful, lithe (that is, if we're lucky).

And such classifications are certainly not limited to national sports magazines or sponsors. In a review of high school girls' basketball, sports editor Eric Davis of our local *The Marion Star* (Marion, OH) wrote: "And, at the risk of sounding sexist, I've got to say that Carrie Carr is just about the prettiest girl I've ever seen on a basketball court.

"I honestly don't watch for such things when I attend girls ball games but I ain't blind, either, don't you know?"[4]

Those who played with or against the pretty Carr were devastated. While girls making lay-ups, rebounds, and three-pointers got no credit at all, Carrie Carr got a full paragraph based on her looks. Worse, in response to the outburst of protest from parents, coaches, fans, and players, Davis wrote a lengthy defense of his job, ending it with "I'm not about to start buddying up to board members or engaging in some other sort of sneaky, behind-the-scenes endeavor to obtain undue influence. . . . I'll leave all that stuff to impatient, and usually ignorant, fans, plus that frightening minority — and let's hope it stays a minority — of nagging, meddling, judgmental, jealous, unrealistic, and overprotective parents."[5]

Yikes.

We have learned something about beauty from our male interviewees, too. While the non-athletic young men favored Pamela Anderson Lee of "Baywatch," the athletic males preferred athletes such as Gabrielle Reece "any day of the week."

For example, there is Rob Blevis, the stud of Accelerate Ohio, running 22 miles per hour, with a sculpted body. We admit we had him figured for a guy who would go for the head cheerleader.

We were wrong. "I would want to go out with someone like Gabrielle," Rob says. "She's got nice muscles. You can tell she'd be a lot more fun. We would have a lot more in common. She respects herself, she's dedicated, she probably has a lot better work ethic than some girl just trying to run around being pretty."

Certainly beauty is in the eye of the beholder. But in the sports world many seem to believe that the "beholders" prefer white, early-twenties females. While no one questions the amazing feats of Mary Lou Retton, one has to wonder why until 1996 she was the only female to grace the cover of the Wheaties box. What about Jackie Joyner-Kersee, the greatest female athlete alive? "Unfortunately, African-American women will never get as much spotlight as white women," says Wyomia Tyus, who returned from the 1964 Mexico City Olympics as the first person ever to win a gold medal in the 100 meters in two consecutive Olympic Games (a feat not repeated until Carl Lewis did it two decades later). But an African-American woman, she was a product of her time; there were no endorsements awaiting her.

Mary Lou Retton

Wendy Hilliard, nine-time member of the National Rhythmic Gymnastics team and former president of the Women's Sports Foundation, attests to Tyus' feelings. As the only African-American team member, Hilliard often felt different. "We would compete in Poland and I'm sure I was the only black person in the whole country. Little kids would come up to me and say, 'chocolate'." Hilliard learned to deal with it with humor. "I'd say, 'When I leave, *allll* your entertainment is gonna be gone.'"

And as far as the popularity of Gabrielle Reece, Hilliard acknowledges: "Things aren't always even on the playing field, or in the marketing field. It comes down to who the public wants to see. There are more accomplished athletes than [Reece], but she's got everything that is comfortable for middle America." She's muscular, without being too much of a jock. (She plays on a four-woman team, rather than an Olympic-caliber two-woman team.) Volumes of hair, slender, tall, and glamorous.

Wyomia Tyus is all too familiar with this societal pressure. Like other female athletes before her and since not from middle America, Tyus faced the issue of the appropriate feminine image. She was always asked why she was running, training so hard, and moving into a then male-dominated arena. She was warned that if she kept it up she would "get muscles and never be able to get a husband."

Mildred "Babe" Didrikson-Zaharias, labeled by the Associated Press the "Greatest Athlete of her Era" and the "Outstanding Woman Athlete of the Century" (in 1950), also battled society's perceptions of proper feminine behavior. At the qualifying event for the 1932 Olympic Games, Didrikson-Zaharias entered, as a one-woman team, eight events and won five — the shotput, eighty-meter hurdles, javelin throw, broad jump, and baseball throw — outscoring the entire 22-member second-place team of the University of Illinois (Urbana). She qualified for six individual events for the 1932 Games in Los Angeles, but Olympic rules at the time forced her to choose only three. She won two gold medals in the javelin and 80-meter hurdles and a silver in the high jump, setting new world records with almost every effort. She would have won the gold, rather than silver, in the high jump but the judges ruled her jumping style illegal; her head preceded her body and legs over the bar (which is how athletes jump today).

After the Olympics, Didrikson-Zaharias toured the country pitching for an all-male baseball team, shooting with an all-male basketball team, and boxing against men. In April 1935, she won the Texas Women's Golf Association Amateur championship, but the United States Golf Association (USGA) declared her a professional athlete because of her years of exhibition touring. She was heavily ridiculed for her tomboyish manners and style, for her short-cropped hair, lack of make-up, and flamboyant showmanship. And it was made very clear to her that she was not welcome at such socially-elite functions as golf tournaments.

So while awaiting reinstatement of her amateur status, Didrikson-Zaharias took up sewing, gardening, and housewifely duties. Not until she grew her hair out and began curling it, wore make-up, and polished her nails did she gain the kind of acclaim she deserved for her athletic abilities. After three years of waiting, she finally was awarded her new status. In 1946 she won the National Women's Amateur title, and in 1947 she went on to win 17 straight amateur victories — a feat still unequaled, even by Tiger Woods. She turned pro in 1948 and won 33 professional tournaments, including three U.S. Opens.

Didrikson-Zaharias went on to be the driving force behind the creation of the Ladies Professional Golf Association. In her career she won, over a forty-year period, more medals and tournaments and set more records in more sports than any other twentieth-century athlete — of either sex.[6] But the lesson for all women athletes was clear: you won't be allowed to succeed unless you look and act the way a woman should. And female athletes remain caught between those two still contradictory roles: settle for "you throw like a girl" comments, which mean you're a lesser athlete but appropriately female, or risk "you throw like a boy" compliments, which mean you're a superior athlete but a lesser athlete.

Ahhh, the price of beauty.

Let's face it: it's hard to summon the strength and courage to be a storm when being a flower is so much easier and so much more rewarding. Or is it?

We know we've said this before, but it bears repeating: girls who do not participate in sports, who bend to what society seems to want from them, not only have lower self-esteem and self-confidence, but are far more likely to drop out of school, abuse drugs and alcohol, and have unwanted pregnancies. And there are even greater repercussions. Girls who do not participate in sports are far more likely to suffer from depression, exhaustion, and chronic illness, and they are at greater risk of suicide.

But things are improving, and will continue to improve as more and more women enter the field of sports — either as executives, commentators, or athletes. The growing number of women in positions of influence and authority is helping to redefine perceptions of femininity and acceptable feminine behavior. Now, happily, our female athletes are beginning to feel able to present themselves to the sports world and the media just as they are. As Nancy Woodhull pointed out, "The important thing in sports' 'Year of the Women' is that it's very obvious that women have choices they can make. You can succeed on the playing field, on the side-lines, or in the classroom. You can be noticed because you scored in double figures for the basketball team or because you wear short skirts." The Billie Jean Kings, Micki Kings, Donna de Varonas, Wyomia Tyuses, Nancy Lieberman-Clines, and Martina Navratilovas opened the door for us. Many people cite Dorothy Hamill, Chris Evert, and Peggy Fleming as important mediators. At a time when the media and public alike were redefining what was acceptable feminine behavior, these women were soft and pretty, but also serious athletes. Now enter the Tia Trents and Jenna Braders — determined, focused, anything they want to be, redefining femininity, and opening a new door.

But how can we get through to *all* girls that sports are important and positive? How do we get that message through to those girls slighted on the basketball court and in the newspaper? How do we undo insults inflicted by public figures such as New York Jets coach Bill Parcells, who (in 1996, while coaching the New England Patriots) referred to an injured rookie receiver as "she" throughout a press conference, implying that the player was perhaps too delicate for the NFL? How can we override the images of Pamela Anderson Lee and Kate Moss, dispel the words of small-minded sportswriters and sportscasters, and replace them with images of such strong, healthy, beautiful women as Gail Devers, Gwen Torrence, and Mia Hamm? How do we help girls to see and believe that those who participate in sports are happier and more successful? How do we illustrate that athletics (no matter what level) help girls and women find themselves and feel productive, worthwhile, strong? Sports psychologist Pat Bach says that finding themselves allows females to find their "inner-athlete" — the long-suppressed, competitive, resilient, strong-minded being. And when females find that inner athlete, they find their inner beauty.

But, like all quests, the search for that inner beauty is elusive, a road filled with obstacles. And defeating society's image of "proper feminine behavior" and feminine beauty is a problem even in female sports, casting self-doubt among even the strongest of us.

Carol Oglesby, a sport psychologist at Temple University, developed what she terms the "Apologetic Theory," meaning women are permitted entry into the male domain (of sports) providing that they display "proper feminine behavior." Grunting, sweating, pumping iron are frowned upon. But to be an athlete, you have to do these things, so you had better wear make-up while you do it. A nice pair of heels would be good, too. (We all remember Ann Richard's comment about Ginger Rogers: she did everything Fred Astaire did, only backwards and in heels.)

The female athlete is very often considered — by other women, no less — to be less than feminine, less than attractive. The athlete's strength seems to be threatening, disconcerting to women who have never embraced, or even felt, strength. American women still aren't fans of women's sports. They prefer figure skating, where the women don't look like athletes, and gymnastics, where the athletes don't look like women.

No wonder many female athletes struggle with their own and others' perceptions of their femininities. Boxer Christy Martin, along with her husband/trainer, works hard to assure people that she's not a "manly-type woman." During her matches, she wears bright pink and purple eye shadow and rose-colored lipstick to match her pink satin trunks and robe. And after matches, she immediately applies new make-up and slips into a miniskirt for post-match press conferences. She's even considering a *Play-*

boy profile.

Martin wants people to know that she's not particularly interested in women's issues, contending that women should not be police officers or firefighters. "I'm not a pioneer for women's boxing," she says. "I'm not out to make a statement about women in boxing, or even women in sports." Her husband agrees. "She's in the game for herself, not for all women."[7]

Jackie Phelan, inducted into the Mountain Bike Hall of Fame and notorious for her high-speed, daredevil descents from mountaintops, bejewels herself during competitions with plastic costume jewelry and a fake braid that attaches to her baseball cap so that spectators will know she is a woman.

A friend of ours and former teammate worried during our workouts that she was becoming too muscular. A former speedskater, she has beautiful and powerful legs. We have always admired her legs, wishing ours were more like hers. Power, of course, is essential in bobsledding. And, from a non-sports related point of view, her legs are just plain attractive. But she worried that they were "huge" and unappealing, and eventually cut down on the weights so that she wouldn't increase in size.

Angela Bassett's agent told us that Bassett (*What's Love Got To Do With It?* and *Waiting To Exhale*) hates her well-toned arms and does her best to cover them.

Size of muscles seems to be a particularly vexing issue in women's athletics. A slight degree of muscularity is acceptable (Cindy Crawford, for example), but big muscles equate manliness. In the male-dominated sport of bodybuilding where men are rewarded for huge, bulging muscles, the verdict is still out on what the desired female body image is. Athletes are judged on "overall appearance" as well as muscularity and symmetry.

But remember Bev Francis, the brawny New Zealand powerhouse? She never stood a chance. Heads and shoulders above the other contestants, her muscularity and symmetry were perfect. But she was not pretty — the ultimate sin for a woman. Her mousy brown hair, pock-marked face, and large nose outweighed her athletic skill. So she lost to a less muscular, but more "attractive," appropriately feminine contestant.

Enter Cory Everson, the blonde bombshell of the bodybuilding world. Initially, she was criticized for stepping into the male-dominated sport, but Everson confused the "Old Guard." She was sexy. She was bright and positive. She was intelligent. She was determined. And athletically, she was very gifted.

Cory Everson

While Everson continued to train, to shine on the posing stage, it was hard to ignore her. Fans loved her. She was and is a positive role model for young women. (In fact, Everson is one of several sports celebrities who agreed to talk to us even though she has her own book to promote — simply because she believes in the message we are sending.)

Now with her own work-out show on ESPN, a book, and a staff writer position for *Muscle & Fitness*, Everson has dispelled many stereotypes of female athletes. "Fitness," she says, "is sexy for everyone."

Sexy, indeed. While training in the Olympic Training Center weight room, we spied a Cory Everson poster. Actually, it wasn't hard to spy since two speedskaters, a luger, and a trainer were holding it up and evaluating every inch of Cory's well-toned, muscled body.

"You like that?" we asked, feeling out our audience.

"She's *hot*!"

"Yeah," we played devil's advocate, "but she's got all those muscles."

"Yeah, and she looks gooooood!"

When we asked Everson about this, she laughed. The image of women with muscles is a healthy one for men to see. No Kate Moss, she. Everson is a solid, muscular woman who could easily bench press most of the young men who oogle her picture. "Girls can learn from us that having a fit body and fit mind are attractive and feminine," she says.

Alrighty, then. Chalk one up for the athletes. Now, if we could just break through to the television audience. . . .

When the movie "Cagney and Lacey" aired on CBS, very little promotion had been done and, in fact, there were no plans for a series. CBS decision makers concluded that there was not much of a demand for a female partner cop show. Not until feminist Gloria Steinem and actress Loretta Swit appeared on the Phil Donahue show urging viewers to write to CBS did network executives sit up and take notice. Thousands and thousands of letters poured in to CBS demanding a series depicting two women as co-workers and friends.

For decades, women and men have accepted the notion that women cannot work together. And if a woman did venture into a male role in television land, she had to be flanked by men. "Police Woman" and "Mod Squad" starred pretty women who worked side-by-side with men.

Olympic beach volleyball player Angela Rock says this notion about women is a consequence of the perception that the only time women compete against one another is over men. And Rock may be on to something. For so long, women were deprived of the right to play sports. Women who were "catty" about who was prettier, who had the nicer hair or figure, were simply expressing a natural human instinct — competitiveness — in one of the few avenues allowed to them by society. When other avenues, such as sports, are allowed, we see that women can and do work and play together well.

For example, despite the criticism the show provoked, "Charlie's Angels" was actually a step forward for women's images. Hard to believe with as much fluff and cheesecake as appeared in the series, the show was also the first time a popular television show allowed women to be friends, co-workers, and professionals at the same time. The three women never fought; there were no stereotypical cat fights in a pool of water, no hair pulling, no mud wrestling. The characters of "Charlie's Angels" respected and loved each other. They were professional, independent, and doing dangerous work. Okay, the plots left a lot to be desired, and the women were gorgeous, but the scripts allowed women to have healthy, strong relationships without being a pretext for merely fulfilling male sexual fantasies. It was, in that healthy way, real life.

Unfortunately, like the internationally popular "Baywatch," "Charlie's Angels" also carried another message: that little girls should try to live up to an impossible ideal of beauty. "Baywatch" did have the character Stephanie, who is tall, lean, and muscular, but the show's producers killed her character. What does that say about how far we've come?

Women are ready for images of strong, smart women on television. Perhaps that is why the syndicated action-adventure series "Xena" is such a success. In it the heroine, who possesses superhuman strength, battles warriors in the "golden age of myth." In real life, the nearly six-foot tall actress Lucy Lawless says of the show, "It just seems to have hit the world at the right time. The world is ready for a woman hero who is smarter and stronger than she is good-looking. People somehow find her empowering."[8]

Of course, Lawless/Xena is very good-looking and men love her. (In fact the show regularly beats "Baywatch" and "Star Trek: Deep Space Nine" in the ratings.) But it is women who love her most, who have given her unsuspicious and unresentful support. Fan letters, Internet forums and, most recently, *Ms.* magazine have honored Lawless for her portrayal of a superhero. (And her popularity is growing: there are Xena-fests, Xena trading cards, action figures, CD-ROMs, and more than 60 Web sites.) Not only can Xena battle evil, taking down scores of evil warriors, but her best friend and sidekick is named Gabrielle — yes, a woman. And they do kick some serious butt. We like that.

We also like that Peta Wilson of the action-packed, kick-ass show "La Femme Nikita" can punch, kick, and take out a bad guy without batting an eyelash, while remaining the most morally-conscious character on the show.

We are overdue for realistic and positive female role models. It is past time to end women's socially-inflicted anguish over trying to obtain unrealistic (and essentially unimportant) standards of beauty. We need a "revolution in our values,"as Pipher says, about how we define attractiveness. That revolution should begin with women. We need to broaden our own definitions of beauty to include — without succumbing to the usual suspicions and stereotypes — the athletic body.

Hilliard stresses that the recognition women got during the 1996 Olympic Games is only the first step. "The second step is who [i.e., which athletes] we keep out there and how they are portrayed." The Women's Sports Foundation tells us that one of the most frequently asked questions about the media coverage of women's sports is "What is the harm of portraying female athletes as pretty and feminine?" The Foundation's response: images are powerful tools that shape and reflect attitudes and values. By portraying sportswomen either as sex objects or as "pretty ladies," the message is that sportswomen are not strong, powerful, and highly skilled individuals. Ultimately, images that ignore or trivialize females undermine the importance of women's sports and respect for the abilities of female athletes.

Hilliard says, "One thing the Women's Sports Foundation promotes is a healthy body image. While that is important, the one thing we should be focusing on is our *athletic ability*. This is the third step. We're up against something difficult, but if we get more women into marketing and VIP positions, things will change. They will get better."

Only when women have the courage to change their perceptions of beauty and femininity (and ability) will the standards change. Only then will women truly believe in their abilities *and* their own beauty — physical and spiritual. Only then when a female athlete is told, "You throw like a girl," will she be able to answer, "Thank you," and mean it. And only then — for the first time in most women's lives — will the sky be the limit.

And perhaps we'll be able to change the men's perceptions of women along the way. Just as in the story of marathon runner

Patty Driscoll and the truck driver, we cannot assume the worst of our brothers. We must work past that point. If we expect acceptance, equality, and respect, we may just get it.

American Gladiator Shirley "Sky" Eson hits it best when she says: "No one can show you disrespect without your permission. It's up to us to show everyone how beautiful we are. It is what you exude and it all starts in believing in yourself." During breaks in the taping of the Gladiators series, Sky comes out and gives motivational talks to the audience. Sky urges children, particularly young girls (and most especially her two daughters), to believe in themselves. "Everything depends on how much you believe in yourself," she tells kids. "It is the greatest gift to yourself and to the world. Imagine what you can do!"

At 6'3" and 187 pounds, Sky is susceptible to labeling and stereotyping. But to her it doesn't matter. It is what you do with that label that matters. "They call me the Muscular Barbie Doll," she laughs. "I say, that's okay. She's independent, she has a Corvette and a Ferarri, and she's successful. Hey, she only plays with Ken when she wants to and *he* was only brought around for her. I can deal with that!"

We can deal with that, too. And speaking of the Barbie image... we wish that this book could come with a small tape recording so that everyone could hear the words of trainer Radu as he practically yelled at us when asked about women's images and cosmetic surgery.

"We have forgotten what is important," exclaims Radu, his voice rising. "Don't ever be proud of something you can buy! Be proud of the things you do. Be proud of the things you can accomplish. *Make* people respect you. For people who have cosmetic surgery, they don't even understand it's not them. Women's liberation fought so hard. For what? Vanity? It is up to *you* to convince society what you are. You must *do*! Let us judge on what people do. Create! Do! Make things happen! Dream! This is living. But you must work for everything. Don't ever be proud of the things you buy."

It is no wonder that Radu's star pupil echoes his philosophy of physical honesty. How many times have we heard Cindy Crawford say, "I don't look like Cindy Crawford when I wake up in the morning." She expresses concern that teenage girls not be fooled by media images of beauty — citing the hours spent before photo shoots applying dark make-up to her outer thighs and backs of the arms where women normally have fat, and taping her breasts and applying dark make-up to her cleavage to make her breasts appear larger. She is an outspoken beauty, not afraid to disclose her weight — well over 130 pounds — or imperfections.

Tyra Banks, the 1997 cover model for the *Sports Illustrated* swimsuit issue, also acknowledges that modeling is about deception. "We wear hairpieces and all this make-up. And the oil on our bodies reflects muscles that aren't even there. I don't have muscle tone," she says, "but it looks like I do on the cover because of the oil."[9]

In contrast, so many celebrities even deny beauty enhancements and plastic surgery, refusing to be responsible to young females about what is real and realistic beauty. This is why we are proud of Cindy Crawford, who takes this responsibility seriously for her sisters. She is a self-made businesswoman whose candor and honesty have made her likeable and respectable. Whereas *Playboy* is still peddling the Stepford Wives image. For example, in 1997, Farrah Fawcett celebrates turning 50 with a

Playboy Home Video. One of the biggest sex symbols of the second half of this century is being remade by the Playboy folks — to be taller and more buxom than she actually is. As if she isn't sexy enough.

According to a casting notice going around Hollywood in search of a Farrah Fawcett look-alike, the producers are looking for a 5′6", 110-pound model with 34-36 D bust, 25-inch waist, and 36-inch hips. Hello? Does anyone besides us remember Fawcett's scantily-clothed body on "Charlie's Angels" or in her big-selling posters? One hundred and ten pounds and a 36 D bust?! How would she walk?

The women on the U.S. women's bobsled team tease Michelle constantly about her size 6 svelte body (as she is one of the smallest women on the team). At 5′6", Michelle has 36-inch hips and weighs in at 135 pounds. So we must ask ourselves, if Michelle is teased by elite athletes for being "stick woman" at 135 pounds, what would a woman of the same height, but weighing 110 pounds with two watermelons stuck to her chest look like? A chiropractor's dream? An avid *Playboy* reader's fantasy? Or yet another destructive and unrealistic image for young girls?

We all need to look at our *real* accomplishments. We need to rally around all our female athletes and be proud of their successes. We need to embrace our Tia Trents and Jenna Braders. And we need to put an end to preconceived notions of what athletes should look like, should act like. Was Babe Didrikson-Zaharias less of an athlete or a woman because she didn't wear make-up? Of course not.

But the prejudice can work both ways. We must also accept that in the world of the media, in the corporate marketing strategy, beauty is frequently as important as athletic ability.

Woodhull asked, "Is Lisa Leslie any less of a basketball player because she also can have a career as a model?"

Um, no. The Leslie we saw was grunting, sweating, and hustling the ball like nobody's business. The Leslie we know can dunk, pass, and shoot like a champion.

"Is a beach volleyball player less of an athlete because she plays in a bikini?"

Um, no. Nancy Reno is an animal on the beach. She grunts, sweats, spikes, drives, rallies, and bullies with incredible force and determination.

And about Gabrielle Reece, Woodhull said, "In my opinion, Gabrielle Reece has done a lot for the self-esteem of countless young women simply because she has been able to parlay athletic ability and a six-foot-two-inch, 180-pound body into a role as sex symbol for Generation Xers. As long as marketeers are convinced sex sells — and they are — I don't think we can get away from good-looking men and women dominating the commercial endorsement field."

Okay, but we can and must expand what (and who) is considered beautiful; we can help define our own images. We need more women with the confidence and inner beauty of women like Sky, Nancy Reno, and basketball star Sheryl Swoopes. On a recent airplane trip, Swoopes was asked by a flight attendant if she is a model. "No," she replied, "I'm a basketball player."

"Oh, you don't look like a basketball player."

Swoops asked, "What does a basketball player look like?"

Exactly.

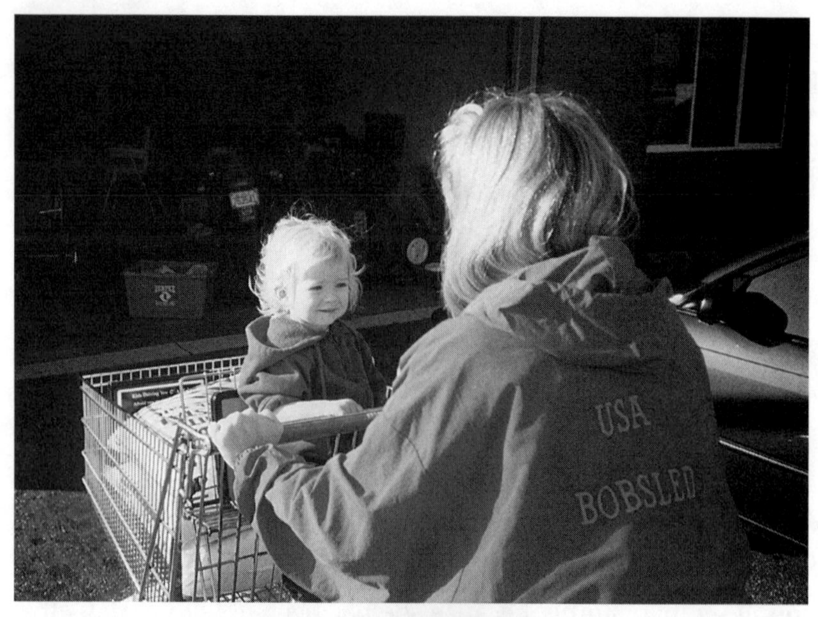

What does a bobsledder look like? Sometimes exactly like a woman at the grocery store. Author Alex, while pregnant, practiced for the bobsled tryouts by pushing her daughter Kerri and 400 pounds of rock salt and weight in shopping carts up slopes.

Chapter Four

The Athlete Within

Honor should not go only
to those who have not fallen.
Rather, honor should go to those
who have fallen, and rise again.
-unknown author

Every successful athlete, success being measured individually by goals set and results attained, has been in the "zone," the point at which her mind and body work together and everything else falls into place. An athlete is more than a person with a special ability and a strong body; she is also a person with a strong mind. Being the strongest or the fastest is not enough — a successful athlete must have the will to prevail, the will to succeed.

Will is what carries athletes through pain and disappointment. It is what picks us up when we have fallen, what carries us toward our goals. It is will that drives us to be dedicated and successful athletes, students, businesswomen, and mothers.

Sometimes women are already accomplished athletes when injuries occur, i.e., Jackie Joyner-Kersee, Mary Decker Slaney, and Kerri Strug, and they must will their bodies to fight weakness and vulnerability. Sometimes the injuries come before great accomplishments. In this chapter, the reader meets women who have overcome terrific odds, often defying disease, debilitating injuries, or trauma to become athletes or to remain athletes.

Wilma Rudolph, for example, overcame severe childhood illnesses that threatened to paralyze her. At age four, Rudolph was struck with polio, scarlet fever, and double pneumonia, and lost the use of her left leg. She walked with a brace or an orthopedic shoe until she was 11 years old, yet nothing could keep her from becoming the world's fastest woman.

For two years, Rudolph's mother drove her 60 miles for physical therapy, and every night her 10 brothers and sisters took turns massaging Rudolph's leg until she was able to walk with a brace. At age eight, she was fitted with an orthopedic shoe to help her walk more normally. By the time she was 11, Rudolph had discarded the shoe to play basketball with her brothers.

She played basketball and ran track through high school and college. While still a high school student, she won a bronze medal at the 1956 Olympic Games as a member of the U.S. 4x100 relay team. In 1960, at the Rome Olympics, Rudolph became the first American woman to win three gold medals in track and field (the 100-meter, the 200-meter, and the 4x100 relay), and she did it with a severely sprained ankle. Labeled "the Gazelle," "the Black Pearl," and "beauty in motion," Rudolph's amazing accomplishments popularized women's track and opened the door for the female athletes who followed.

Venus Lacey, a member of the gold medal women's basketball team at the 1996 Atlanta Games, also overcame childhood disabilities and prognoses that she would never walk without a limp. As a small child, Lacey's brother carried her everywhere because she could not walk unassisted. But Lacey was determined that she would not only walk, she would run and jump. And, indeed, she soared.

In 1988, Gail Devers, fighting Graves Disease, came within one week of having her feet amputated; a change in medication turned things around and saved Devers' athletic career. She says, "Deep within, I was scared to death that I was finished as an athlete."[1] Instead of giving in, she fought back to become the Olympic champion of the 100-meter race in 1992 and 1996.

Recognized as the greatest female athlete of the second half of the 20th century, Jackie Joyner-Kersee has battled injuries (particularly a recurring hamstring injury) and asthma throughout her career to set world records in the long jump and grueling seven-event heptathlon; obtain four Olympic gold medals, one silver medal, and one bronze; and participate in four Olympic Games.

Gymnast Dominique Dawes has also fought through a career of injuries — stress fractures in her foot and wrist, and serious shoulder injuries — to participate in two consecutive Olympics (Barcelona in 1992, Atlanta in 1996), winning a gold medal and two bronzes.

U.S. soccer player Michelle Akers battled debilitating chronic fatigue syndrome during her career with the U.S. team, which won gold at the Atlanta Games. Now, she is gearing up for the first U.S. women's pro league scheduled to begin in 1998.

Mary Ellen Clark overcame bouts of terrifying vertigo to continue diving from a three-story platform and, consequently, win two back-to-back bronzes in platform diving (Barcelona and Atlanta). She refused to walk away when the vertigo seemed insurmountable. "No regrets," she said at the Atlanta Games. "I want to be able to say that in the end. And I can't if I'm walking away because that's quitting. And I'm not a quitter."

In retrospect, she says, "In a strange way vertigo, I think, has made me a better diver, a calmer and more focused athlete. It's given me a greater appreciation for the blessings I've had in my sport, and helped me see that life is more than competition and diving."[2] Clark is now giving motivational speeches, hoping other women can learn from her. "If people I know get discouraged, I tell them to look at me," she says. "I'm a living example that the impossible is possible. I've been down so many times, but I've been able to get back up. And so can they."[3]

Six-time Ms. Olympia Cory Everson entered a terrifying world of paralysis due to a blood clot. Everson suffered from what could be compared to a stroke, losing the ability to walk, talk and even feed herself. While we spoke with Everson, we found her incredibly inspiring as she spoke candidly about re-learning to feed herself. Always determined she could do it and return to athletics, Everson persisted. "Physical fitness and sport are so important for taking control of your own life and never giving up again," she says.

While Everson quietly serves as a role model for so many breaking into the world of weightlifting and bodybuilding, few can imagine her personal struggle to simply stand again.

The world of sport is filled with stories of athletes who have overcome handicaps and dealt with pain. Co-author and bobsledder Michelle Powe is another one of those athletes. Literally incapacitated by a car accident in 1993, Michelle — already an asthmatic — spent a year bed-ridden, suffering tremendous head pain, unable to work or even function well from day-to-day. Since the accident, she has undergone a series of surgeries and countless tests and treatments, seen countless doctors, and become an expert on the subject of pain management.

Despite her constant, severe pain, Michelle decided in 1994 that she had to "get back in the game." It was the occasion of the first try-outs for the U.S. women's bobsled team that was her "coming out." She joined that special group of women who were the first-ever American women's team in the sport of bobsled.

Michelle's constant pain is still with her. But instead of accepting it and letting it defeat her, Michelle excels in spite of her pain. She was the first U.S. women's national champion (1995), and one of the first two U.S. women bobsled drivers to compete internationally. Without a coach, the proper equipment or, really, an idea of what they were doing, four U.S. women competed in St. Moritz, Switzerland — the first time U.S. women had ever competed in international competition.

Valerie Still

In 1991, Valerie Still, a professional basketball player, was involved in a near-fatal automobile accident. While driving, Still was cut off by a speeding car, causing her to lose control of her own car. Still confesses that she, too, was driving at a high speed and, as a result, lost control. Her car swerved off the road and into a tree, crushing Still. Her face was broken, her nose virtually torn from her face. She suffered a broken wrist, cuts and gashes all over her body, but these injuries were the least of her problems. Her pelvis was shattered, broken in six places. Her first vertebrae was fractured, causing doctors to believe she would never walk again, much less play basketball.

Like so many of the women who grace these pages, Still defied medicine. Today she walks and plays with, literally, the best of them. In fact, she was the ABL championship series' Most Valuable Player in the Columbus Quest's victory over the Richmond Rage (now the Philadelphia Rage) in 1997.

Canadian rower Silken Laumann is another striking example of an athlete who has overcome pain to succeed, to mount an inspirational comeback from injury.

In 1992, Laumann was preparing for a competition in Germany when another boat unexpectedly cut across her path. The boat's bow ripped into Laumann's right calf, mangling her leg. Nerves were shredded, muscles badly torn, and her fibula fractured. Her leg required nearly constant attention, with six changes of dressings every day for the next five weeks.

Less than a month after the disastrous accident, Laumann was back in training. She pointed out to those who tried to stop her that there were only 78 days left before the Olympic trials. Daily training meant rolling her wheelchair to her shell and crawling into the scull; but she did it, and she made it through the trials. Then, Laumann showed everyone her athlete within; she pulled on everything she had and won the bronze medal in Barcelona.

Laumann's leg has not regained its original shape and strength, her ankle still swells, her balance is unreliable, and the pain is always with her. And what is this great athlete's response? She took a silver medal at the 1996 Olympic Games in Atlanta.

Joan Benoit Samuelson had arthroscopic surgery on her knee seventeen days before the 1984 Olympic trials for the first women's marathon in Olympic history. She began training five days after surgery, but because she was compensating for her injured right leg, she pulled her left hamstring. It seemed too much to overcome, yet she would not quit. On the morning of the Olympic trials, Benoit Samuelson decided to start the race and run as far as she could. She won the trials, and went on to win the Olympic marathon itself. Many women before her had laid the groundwork for this day — women like Roberta Gibb Bingay, who in 1966 was the first woman to run in the Boston Marathon (she wore a hooded sweatshirt to disguise her appearance since women were not allowed), and Kathrine Switzer, who ran in the 1967 Boston Marathon (she used her initials when signing up) and was accosted by a race official trying to prevent her from running. "To see a woman run [the Olympic marathon] with such courage and brilliance showed the world that women, too, can be heroes," Switzer says.[4]

Such women demonstrate that sport actively gives health, channels energies in positive ways, and allows people a means for overcoming handicaps that might otherwise overcome them.

The power of the will to persevere, the will that makes a winner, is demonstrated by Ana Fidelia Quirot, Cuban 800-meter runner. Quirot became a runner in an unusual way. She incorrectly was identified as a child with learning disabilities and sent to a special school. It was there that a coach saw her racing barefoot and recognized the athlete within.

And what an athlete she is: two gold medals at the 1987 Pan Am Games; a bronze at the 1992 Barcelona Olympics (in spite of a leg injury, being pregnant, and mourning the recent death of her friend and trainer); and silver medals at the 1994 Central American Games, the 1996 World Championships, and the Atlanta Games. The last three victories were won following a disastrous kitchen fire that engulfed the upper half of Quirot's body, leaving her with third-degree burns, and resulted in the premature birth and subsequent death of her baby. The doctors did not tell Quirot of her baby's death for many days. As Quirot herself clung to life, they were sure the news would kill her. Despite months of surgery, Quirot has restricted head and arm movement, a handicap that she is determined to defeat just as she has beaten lesser injuries and overcome poverty and the trauma of her child's death.

In the races that followed the tragedy, Quirot shocked the medical community by running. Each time she ran, she cracked and split healing skin. Many of the medical staff who treated Quirot burst into tears when they watched her racing on television, not because they were happy for her, but because they knew the new level of pain she had reached by splitting the healing skin. It was extraordinarily painful, but Quirot persisted to win a silver at the Atlanta Games.

"What helped me rehabilitate quickly," she says, "was going back to sports. Many people believed that was impossible. But if I had not started running again, I believe I would have died. It was what kept me alive."[5]

Perhaps of all the athletes we had the pleasure of meeting, we were most touched by Barbara Underhill, a Canadian pair's figure skater. Anyone who loves ice dancing knows Barbara. She and skating partner Paul Martini perform fast-paced, steamy, on-the-edge-of-your-seat dance routines that wow their audiences. Happily married, mother of beautiful twin girls, Canada's sweetheart, she was on top of her game. But on May 29, 1994, tragedy struck. Two-year-old twin Stephanie Underhill drowned. "Our whole lives were turned upside down," says Barbara. "I didn't think I would be able to skate again. I just thought, 'How could I ever feel joy again? Smile again? How could I do anything?'"

Slowly, Barbara found her way back to the ice. "It felt strange at first. Then, it began to be a release. When you are grieving constantly and it is the constant thought in your head and it surrounds you, you need an outlet. That's what skating was for me. I would be on the ice and just cry and scream and get out all my emotions. Other days, I would find myself actually smiling and I would suddenly realize what was happening to me. Skating was a big help. It became my therapy. Skating at that point in my life was what I needed most. Paul and I skated through that season. I think back on it now, but I can't really remember it very well. But it was there for me."

The stories that inspire and humble us go on. Triathlete Suzann Mouw is a formerly nationally-ranked athlete who is continuing her sport while she fights a recurring form of Hodgkin's disease.

Paralympian runner Sara Reinertsen, born without a left leg and told she could not run, is a world record holder in the women's 100-meter dash for above-the-knee amputees. Reinertsen is also responsible for introducing a leg-over-leg method of running that has become popular with the best amputee athletes. (The leg-over-leg running style is faster, but requires extraordinary strength and coordination.)

Wheelchair racer Linda Mastandrea has triumphed on the track and in the law, simultaneously setting world records and graduating from law school. She is currently a practicing attorney with world records in the 100-meter, 200-meter, and 400-meter races. Participating in the Atlanta Games was particularly sweet for Mastandrea, who also went to the Barcelona Games — and learned upon arrival in Spain that she would not be racing because her events did not have enough participants to be included in the Games.

In the 1996 Atlanta Paralympic Games, Mastandrea won the gold in the 200-meter race, again showing the world her tremendous will to win (in all ways).

In 1990, Karen Gardner was a competitive gymnast and track and field athlete (and a recreational skier) with a history of orthopedic knee problems when she began complaining of pain in her left knee. Her doctor blamed the pain on scar tissue from multiple surgeries, and disregarded her concerns. But, in fact, Gardner had bone cancer, and had to have her left leg amputated to save her life (after finally insisting on a diagnosis from another doctor).

As she left the hospital, just having been informed of the large, malignant mass behind her knee, Gardner kicked her bad leg with the good and said to her mother, "Well, at least I can ski again." And ski she did. Six months after the surgery, she learned again how to ski, and is now the world champion in the disabled super giant slalom.

We have met so many brave and persevering athletes, and have heard about countless more. We never cease to marvel at the remarkable strength of the human spirit. One of our favorite sources of motivation is champion bodybuilder and former member of the first all-women America Cup crew, Shelley Beattie (aka "Siren" of the "American Gladiators"). Beattie has overcome numerous obstacles — from uncaring foster parents and the special disability of a hearing loss to physical injuries and mental depression.

Beattie's severe hearing loss made her an unusual crew member for America[3] and set up new challenges for her and her teammates. But Beattie has frequently been in first-ever circumstances and has paid the price.

She talks about being the first and only girl in her school to go near the weight room. At fourteen years of age, Beattie wanted to do some lifting to help her gain weight for the track season. She says, "People thought I was weird for [weightlifting]. And especially when I quit track after my junior year in high school to become a bodybuilder!

"A few years later, I became a pro. Then, 1992 was my first year with the 'American Gladiators.' In 1995, I made the first all-woman America's Cup sailing team. [Have I been] criticized? [Have I been] ridiculed? That's like asking if the Pope's Catholic."

Beattie is unusual in another way: she has accomplished most of her goals alone. Now she has the strong support of her husband, John, who encouraged her to try out for the women's America's Cup crew. But John was not there when Beattie was growing up the hard way, in a series of foster families who didn't have time for or interest in the ambitions of a developing athlete. By the time Beattie was 17, she was on her own, supporting herself and finishing high school. She kept right on working for the next four years while going to college and training as a bodybuilder. She says that throughout the years, there were always one or two people who were friends, people "who accepted me and tried to understand me, no matter how closed I was at the time." Those are the people she credits with helping her by believing in her just enough to let her believe in herself. (As Bonnie Blair says, "One person believing in you can give you great power, even if that one person is yourself.")[6]

In 1990, Beattie won the USA bodybuilding championship and a contract with a major vitamin supplement company. She was in the limelight more and more, not an easy thing for a woman who is naturally withdrawn. For Beattie, the bright side to her growing fame has been the children who are her fans. She hopes she is helping them by being a good role model. "I love the letters I get from children and parents of deaf kids. I always send them free photos and a reply of thanks. I love to go to deaf and hearing schools to 'talk' with the kids. I can't explain how good that makes me feel. I think it helps me more than it helps them," she says.

Prior to making the America[3] crew, Beattie had never been a team member. Combined with her hearing loss, that made for some uneasy times in the beginning. "At first, being on a team with all hearing women, I was very frustrated and angry with myself. Teamwork requires good communication and keeping up. I had to confront many issues — especially those relating to my hearing loss — for the first time in years.

"In college, I had a sign language interpreter for meetings, social functions, and TV interviews, but on the boat it was just me and my teammates. I taught them some basic signs for 'grind' and 'stop,' and also ways to get my attention, like tap me on the shoulder, wave to me, or stomp on the floor. The grinders asked me to teach them more sign language, so we all could talk to each other from a distance and in social settings.

"In the end, this was the best experience I've ever had — belonging to a group. My deafness forced me to confront and deal with real life without hiding it or pretending it's not important."

Beattie has had to confront other issues during her athletic career. Being a female bodybuilder, especially one of national note, makes her a person who stands out, who looks different. When we asked Beattie about the feminine models that society promotes to young women, she responded, "I don't pay attention to what other people define as 'feminine' or 'masculine' because I've always felt everyone has both. And nobody I've met has a perfect balance of the two. I've never been one to follow what the media defines as feminine."

Because of her personal independence and her athletic choices, Beattie says she has never been perceived as "normal" in lifestyle or in physical appearance. "When I made the all-women sailing team, some of the women just stood and stared at me in the locker room. My best friend, Amy, told me once that it's because no one has ever seen a body like mine. I asked her if that was bad. She said no, but they still don't know what to think of it. As a professional bodybuilder, I have always been stared at and [had] comments [made] behind my back, some positive and some negative. Ignorant people are everywhere. I try not to interpret how others see me or I may become the idea of what they think I am. I don't let others define who I am or label me. I am only concerned [about] my image for the children's sake."

"For the children's sake." That statement is a sure sign of a female role model. And Beattie's role models? They are Jackie Joyner-Kersee and Cory Everson. Beattie considers herself fortunate to have one of her role models, Everson, as a good friend.

When we asked Beattie about the benefits of athletics, she knew exactly what she wanted to say: "Through athletics, I have gained self-esteem and value in myself. I would not be here today if I [hadn't had] sports to turn to. The older and more experienced I've gotten, [the more] my 'shell' has softened, and it has helped me be less fearful of failure and making mistakes — like the time I froze on stage in the middle of my routine because I looked at the audience and lost the beat.

"[Athletics has] continually challenged me to push past my mental and physical limits, having to go past my pain threshold over and over again, recovering from mental [defeats and physical] injuries. . . . Trying to prove to myself that I have worth, that I have inner strength to overcome any obstacle.

"As my hearing worsened, I became more hard on myself and, several times, I pushed myself to the edge. Athletics has always been a way for me to release buried anger and frustration. That may sound negative, but what I mean to say is sports benefit women in so many ways. . . . Women learn to communicate emotions and learn leadership skills. . . . Team sports help women to make quick decisions and learn self-control and discipline. . . . Sports will help an introverted and withdrawn person to be more aggressive and outgoing. All women should feel in control of their destiny and empowered [to act]."

The benefits of sports are so varied; they can help us overcome so many obstacles life throws before us. Will. Determination. Courage. Empowerment. The women in this chapter show us that pain and injuries often go beyond the physical, but that women have the strength and fortitude to endure and achieve and become even stronger. They show us that there is hope for those who suffer all types of pain, and that winning comes in different forms. High jumper Louise Ritter expressed best the feelings of the athlete within: "It's about the challenge, the journey — all the stuff we learn about the sport, ourselves, and the confidence-building that goes along with it. Even if you never reach your dream, you still learn something from the process."

Chapter Five

Are You a Mother or an Athlete?

Give birth to me, sisters, in struggle we transform
ourselves, but how often, how often
we need help to cut loose, to cry out, to breathe!...
This morning we must make each other strong.
Change is qualitative: we are
each other's miracle.

— Marge Piercy

In 1994, at the first try-outs for a U.S. women's bobsled team, the culmination of the competition was the push championship. The competitors pushed a 325-pound sled on a rubberized track (the equivalent of a 450-pound sled on ice) for 50 meters, going as fast as they could go. The top eight finishers made the team.

At the time, Alex was 29 years old and four months pregnant with her second child. She won the championship. The woman who placed second, Liz Parr-Smestad, was 32 years old and three months pregnant with her first child. Both women had planned their pregnancies so that they would sit out the first season, but have their babies in plenty of time to get back into shape and return for the following year's nationals and subsequent season.

Despite the fact that Alex and Liz proved themselves worthy athletes, despite the fact that they trained as hard (or harder) than their teammates, they were informed by a major player in the bobsled federation that they would have to choose between the roles of motherhood and athlete. "Are you a mother or an athlete?" he asked? Two years later, the new team director told Alex and Liz that he was counting them out as competitive team members because they are mothers.

Such unfair treatment is not unique to bobsledding. We have traditionally placed a burden of confusion on mothers in society-at-large and particularly on mother-athletes. The message is to be nurturing, caring, loving, and all-giving; just don't bother having outside dreams or aspirations. But how can mothers without dreams and aspirations inspire and encourage their children — boys and girls — to aspire and to succeed?

While more than 100 athletes are listed with the USOC as parents, just over a dozen are mothers. Small wonder. Child care alone is a logistical and financial nightmare. And society's questions and doubts remain. "How can she neglect her baby to train?" "How can a woman whose body has endured pregnancy and childbirth still be strong enough to compete?" But anyone who has experienced childbirth knows just how strong you have to be. In fact, during the filming of *Courage Under Fire*, Meg Ryan proved the point to a reporter. During a break, crew members and actors were swapping war stories, showing off scars and wounds. Ryan piped

Alex Powe-Allred

up, "'I had an 11-pound baby.' After that," she says, "everyone shut up."

There are some amazing athlete-mothers who should have been able to put doubts to rest. For example, Fanny Blankers-Koen, a Dutch sprinter, became the first mother to compete in the Olympics and win — winning four gold medals at the 1948 Olympic Games. She was 30 years old, already the mother of two daughters, and three months pregnant at the time of the Olympics. In 1958 (two years before she would win three gold medals at the Rome Games), Wilma Rudolph became pregnant. Tennessee State University had a strict policy against allowing anyone with children to participate in the school's athletic program. Rudolph had no college degree, no husband, no job, and a child on the way. And the 1950's were a tough time for a single African-American woman. But Tennessee State track coach Ed Temple took a chance. Rather than ostracize her, the team and coach rallied to help her. The results, of course, were phenomenal, leading to prestigious athletic and business careers and, eventually, the Wilma Rudolph Foundation (established in 1981).

Others have followed in her footsteps: Valerie Brisco-Hooks (track and field), who says motherhood helped her improve as an athlete; Dorothy Odam Tyler (track and field); Mary Decker Slaney (track and field); Joan Benoit Samuelson (marathon); Olga Appell (marathon); and Elaine Cheris (fencing) all became credible mother-athletes, and championed the notion that pregnancy and motherhood actually improved their performances.

American Gladiator Sky was, at the time of her first child's delivery, a distance cyclist. Indeed, she was cycling when she went into labor, 35 miles outside the city. "I had to decide, hmmm, do I want to stop and call someone or should I ride back into town." She pedaled herself to the hospital.

During her second pregnancy, Sky was leg-pressing 1,000 pounds when she went into labor. She had her baby on Friday and resumed her workout routine on Monday.

Although Alex won the U.S. Bobsled Push Competition when she was four months pregnant, she wasn't doing anything nearly so vigorous at nine months. In fact, she was vacuuming when labor started, which she promptly stopped when the pain became too intense and was driven (in a car) to the hospital. Oh well, we can't all be Superwoman.

Ranked fifteenth in the world in marathon and twentieth in the 10K, Olga Appell is raising a nine-year-old daughter. Appell feels that her greatest sacrifice has been leaving her daughter to travel and compete. "Being a mother and an athlete is difficult," she says about deciding how to train and divide her time. "The fun things are difficult." Appell must balance herself between being a mother, wife, homemaker, and full-time athlete. These things, she stresses, are very important to her, but very taxing. "I feel bad sometimes," she says, when asked how she manages everything. Sacrifice, she says, is the key ingredient to success. Everything has to give a little. Somehow she manages. "My career gives me a lot of satisfaction, but it is more important to be a good mother." And part of being a good mother means fighting for what you believe in, pursuing your dreams, teaching your children to pursue theirs. So, it is also hard to be a good mother, Appell says. A sentiment shared by every mother whether she works outside or inside her own home, whether she works in a gym or in an office.

Olympian Elaine Cheris, ranked third in the world in fencing, has a seven-year-old son. Cheris qualified for the Pan Am Games, and the 1984, 1988, and 1996 Olympics. She manages to hold down the jobs of athlete, mother, fencing club coach, and writer (a book on fencing). Having once trained six to eight hours a day, her lifestyle and training have changed since 1988. "You have to decide what your priorities are, what you want, and how close you can come to these goals," Cheris says. "But there are other factors involved, more important than your sport. How good you are with your child is more important. If he is sick, or having a bad time in school, I miss out on training."

A torn cartilage in her shoulder knocked Cheris out of international competition in 1994. Doctors gave her only a 10 percent recovery chance, but when her son told her he wanted to see her in the 1996 Games, Cheris set her sights on one more challenge. So she began training four to six hours a day, and qualified for the 1996 Atlanta Games, as the oldest American Olympian at the Games.

At the age of fifty, Cheris is back. She is turning a lot of her energies to coaching youngsters at the national level, and she is teaching her son important lessons about determination. He'll be able to say, "My mom did things that weren't particularly easy. Maybe I can, too!" Cheris feels that teaching her son discipline, dedication, and persistence will make him a stronger, happier person.

As to the question of how she managed to compete while caring for a baby and toddler, Cheris laughs. "I never had a babysitter." Cheris simply took her son with her to all of her competitions, and the judges at these events had to learn how to stick a pacifier in his mouth while she competed. "I'm sure some were annoyed," Cheris says of the judges, "but my attitude was you either get both of us, or neither." And since she is one of the United States' greatest fencers, who was going to argue?

Cheris was not alone in bringing her child with her for training and competitions. Nearly 50 years ago, sprinter Blankers-Koen could be seen wheeling her baby stroller into the arena before a meet. Parking her baby at the side of the track, Blankers-Koen got down to business, dominating the world of women's track.

Michelle Rohl, a race walker from Georgia, has double the trouble raising two children. Having trained throughout both pregnancies, Rohl now has a three-year-old son and a six-year-old daughter. At the 1994 Goodwill Games, Rohl came in as the fastest American woman, setting the women's national record at 44:41 for the 10K (6.2 miles). Still, Rohl is sure she can do better. "The hardest part," Rohl says, "is finding the time. I lack the recovery period." Unlike her European competitors, Rohl does not have the luxury of properly cooling down with massage treatments or whirlpools. "I can't do nearly what they do," she says. "I skip cool downs to be with my kids." To make matters more difficult, Rohl's husband also is a competitive athlete, and is a part-time graduate student. The search for money and time are a continuous battle for these two athletes. The Rohls find babysitters wherever they can so that they might train. They are hoping for a grant from the United States Olympic Committee for help. Rohl is sure that given the same amount of quality training time that most of her European competitors have, she would be a world contender.

She already is. At the 1995 Pan Am Games, Rohl went into the race with a diaphragm infection. Both Rohl and her coach Mike Dewitt were unsure if she should compete. Not only did she compete, she won the silver medal. DeWitt says, "Michelle is perhaps one of the most talented athletes I've ever met." When Rohl qualified and then raced in the 1992 Olympic Games, it was only her tenth race ever! At 4'11" and 90 pounds, she quickly became a force to reckon with. Nevermind that she was juggling travel, training, and motherhood. In the spring of 1996, Rohl walked her personal best at 44:06. For this, Rohl credits her family. With strong support from her husband Mike, also a race walker, Rohl believes motherhood has actually made her a better athlete. "My coach always tells me to give 100 percent. I do with both; I try to be as good a mother as I am a race walker. For me, it makes me a better mother because it gives me an outlet."

And Rohl jokes that going through childbirth has made her a tougher athlete. "Nothing can hurt that much," she says. Many other mother-athletes are quick to agree. Indeed, Rohl says she thinks of each oncoming hill as a contraction, "and I say to myself, no hill can ever be *that* hard."

When asked about how she divides her time, Rohl is thoughtful. "It just has to be done." Like most other mothers, Rohl admits that her children are her top priority, and also the driving force for her determination and success.

Sandra Farmer-Patrick and husband David share this in common with the Rohls. While the Rohl family are speed walkers, the Patricks are hurdlers, and the proud parents of two-year-old Sierra. For athletes on the track and field circuit, Sierra's little face is a common sight since her parents try to take her to all their competitions.

In fact, Farmer-Patrick told us that she was surprised at what her daughter had picked up at the Games. Sierra, who had just turned two, caught "the fever" in Atlanta, yelling, "Go, USA! Go, USA!," "Go, Jackie!," and "Go, Michael!"

Like Rohl, the Atlanta Games aren't something Farmer-Patrick necessarily wants to talk about. In fact, her story is a Jackie Joyner-Kersee scenario all over. Farmer-Patrick had injured a hamstring only two weeks before the Games. With vigorous rehabilitation, she could only hope it would hold out for her a few more weeks.

It did, until the semi-finals. Although she finished the race and, as always, was a major threat to her competitors, she was forced to withdraw from the final. The pain was too much. "I didn't want to see anyone, talk to anyone. All I wanted to do was go back to the hotel and see Sierra." Sierra was and is Farmer-Patrick's one consolation — her pride and joy.

Like Rohl, Farmer-Patrick firmly believes she is stronger mentally from having a baby. Her training, her timing, her body, and her priorities have changed since having a baby. To continue to compete as a world champion, an elite athlete, Farmer-Patrick has indeed learned to live up to her own words of advice, which are: "Be consistent. If you can do this, you can endure all things."

The road for Farmer-Patrick has been riddled with injuries since her pregnancy. She told us perhaps one of the most difficult things for her to realize was that she couldn't come back and train like she could when she was 16 or 17 years old. While Gwen Torrence agrees with Farmer-Patrick that childbirth made her a stronger competitor, Torrence says the toughness is all in the mind. Physically, pregnancy and childbirth took its toll on her as well. But like so many other athletes, Torrence says mentally she became tougher.

"I just became more determined to win. People who could never beat me on my worst day were beating me," says Torrence about her return to track after having her son. "I didn't realize how hard it would be to come back. I didn't know how hard it would be to lose the weight." In fact, Farmer-Patrick witnessed many races when Torrence was in tears after the race, after more losses.

"I had Manley in 1989," Torrence says. "1990 was a bad season. In '91, I worked so hard, finally placing second in World's. And I kept thinking maybe if I work a little harder, maybe if I train a little harder. . . ."

When Torrence learned that Farmer-Patrick was pregnant, she warned her chief competitor, "It's not gonna be like you think, darlin'."

Because the body changes so much, because of the postpartum depression and weight problems that follow, Torrence says she has witnessed many injuries when women hurry back to intense training after childbirth. "They all got hurt," Torrence sympathized. When Farmer-Patrick saw Torrence again, she said, "Girl, I know how you felt now."

But both Farmer-Patrick and Torrence are perfect examples of incredible mental training. Both maintain that only the proper frame of mind, positive mental attitude, and the will to come back have allowed them to persevere as champions.

For Valerie Still things weren't so simple. Because her pelvic bone was broken in six different places, it did not heal properly. Doctors told her they were afraid she would not be able to have children and, if she could conceive, there might be complications.

But Still was able to get pregnant and continue her workout regimen until the last month of her pregnancy, when she began suffering from hypertension and was ordered to bed for the remainder of the pregnancy. As she says, "I couldn't do anything."

Eight months later, Still was playing with the Columbus Quest while breastfeeding! While so many other players have a pregame ritual — wearing lucky socks, putting on the right sock before the left, taking a nap or a bath — Still nursed little Aaron.

She definitely agrees with Torrence that motherhood has made her more determined. Motherhood "puts everything in perspective," Still says. Torrence lugs along a bicycle and toys so Manley can play at the track while Mommy practices, and Still brings Aaron to team practices.

"The first thing I talked to Coach [Brian Agler] about was Aaron. Can he come to practices? Can he travel with us? Can he go on the plane?"

Does this mean she's less focused as an athlete? No way. Does this mean she's better at handling different responsibilities and time management? You bet your baby booties.

In fact, only hours before a big game against the San Jose Lasers, Aaron fell ill with a temperature of nearly 103 degrees. Still rushed her baby to the doctor. He was suffering from an ear infection and cold. The same cold Still had. But with a head cold and all her motherhood responsibilities, nothing kept her from the game.

For the women of the Columbus Quest, Aaron is their lucky charm. He's just one of the team. "Oh, they love him," Still says proudly of her teammates. "I think he loosens up the team." During an interview with *USA Today*, Still and the reporter were having a discussion off to the side of the court while various members of the team practiced free throws. The technicians were busily working with the stereo system and lights, when all of the sudden the lights went out. For a moment, everyone was in total darkness. Then, thump, a spotlight came on in center court. Loud music began to blare as teammates Shannon "Pee Wee" Johnson and Sonja Tate were "bumpin' and grindin'" in the spotlight with Aaron dancing in between them.

But even with all the support Still receives from her teammates, it is still difficult being both mother and athlete. "Being a mother really wears on you physically, especially when they're infants," Still says.

Add to that the grueling workouts of elite athletes, and you have some very pooped mommies. Because, as Mary Lou Retton says, "Let's face it. Ultimately, the responsibility rests on the woman."

In the midst of the ABL's first playoffs and winning a trip to the championship, Still worried that she was not cooking enough meals for her family. Rohl worries about successfully balancing the roles of full-time mother, full-time athlete, and full-time supporter of her husband's athletic career. She felt very guilty when she qualified for the Atlanta Games and her husband did not. Teammates Liz and Alex constantly battle with their husbands over the financial and familial costs of bobsledding. And almost all the athletes agreed that no matter how supportive their husbands started out, household problems are blamed on their sports. "If you weren't away so much. . . ." or "If you weren't always at the gym. . . ."

So why go through the suffering? Liz and Alex believe they are making a difference for young women and girls (including their own) to have their fair chance in sports such as bobsledding. Still and Cheris hope their determination and success will make their sons appreciate women more.

Sky states emphatically that having children has made her an even tougher athlete. "Nothing drives me more than hearing my kids cheer me on. Having children has made me better because I know I am their role model. I have to inspire them and show them what they are capable of. I want to hear them say, 'That's my mom! I want to be just like her.'"

And, she says, there is a mutual respect building between her and her babies. Her oldest "baby" Ashley, standing 6'4" at the tender age of 13 years, is already a stand-out basketball and volleyball player. While her children never miss a taping of the American Gladiators, Mom never misses her girls' games either. "Then, I can stand on the sidelines, cheer them on and yell, 'That's my girl!'"

U.S. diver Pat McCormick made the U.S. team and competed in the 1956 Melbourne Games just five months after having a baby. Already a gold medalist from the 1952 Games, McCormick was the woman to beat. With a recovery period not long enough for most women to overcome post-partum depression, McCormick was back in top form. Not only did she take the gold, but she beat her competition by a 16.5 margin — the biggest margin ever in Olympic diving. After winning in the springboard competition, she went on to take a gold in the platform as well. Having also earned two gold medals in the 1952 Games, McCormick was the first diver — man or woman — to win the so-called double double.

As female athletes, it is particularly important to show our children that we *can* do anything we set our minds to — that determination is half the battle, and perseverance is the other half. But is it all worth it in the end? Is all this self-sacrifice, stress, and near-exhaustion worth it?

Liz suffered a hard crash in Calgary in November 1994. Cartilage torn from her sternum made lifting or holding almost anything impossible. While teammates had helped Liz with her dinner trays, changing clothes and even packing her suitcase, we could only stand by miserably when Liz tearfully realized she would not be able to pick up her baby when she got home. But Liz refuses to quit because she wants to be able to tell her children that she fought and won an important battle for herself, for women, for her children. After all, commitment is the means to success.

When we called Olga Appell for an interview, her nine-year-old daughter answered the phone. While we waited for Appell to pick up, we asked her daughter, "So, your mom's a runner, huh?"

"Uh huh," she answered, "marathon. And she's the best in the whole world."

That makes up for a whole lot of suffering.

But the stigma of being a mother and full-time athlete is hard for some to take. "Maybe in ten years," Still says hopefully, "women will know they can be professional athletes and mothers at the same time." But, in the meantime, just as society expects the Gabrielle Reeces and Lisa Leslies to be either athletes or models, it expects others to be athletes *or* mothers.

We asked the athlete moms we interviewed for their reactions to the question "Are you a mother or an athlete?" Most choked for a moment, then asked, "Wait? Who asked that question? Did someone actually ask that question?" Then, always, we were given an earful of what they thought about the guy who asked it. Perhaps the best answer came from Wendy Hilliard. She laughed, "Just look at all the athletes who came back stronger after having a baby. Evelyn Ashford, Gwen Torrence. Hellllоо? It's not an issue anymore. That's a limiting statement." Still, the "Old Guard" stands.

There is a particular stigma to being a mother and athlete during the period of pregnancy. Although the notion that pregnant women must remain inactive is *passe* today, *how much* a pregnant woman should do is still largely in question.

Dr. James Clapp, a renowned obstetric researcher at MetroHealth Hospital in Cleveland, Ohio, studies the correlation between athletics and healthy pregnancies. He has examined the intensity of many types of exercise, monitoring pregnant athletes from aerobics dancers to marathon runners. What he has learned is encouraging. Clapp has conducted thousands of case studies on training injuries during pregnancies. While pregnant women's equilibriums do tend to be off (the new shift in weight tends to make women more clumsy), Clapp's research shows that injury rate does not increase during exercise. One reason: Clapp believes that "pregnant women exercise more control and pay more attention to factors that contribute to injury."

Concerns about pre-term labor induced by extreme exercise also have been reduced greatly. Clapp's studies show that exercise does not initiate pre-term labor, and neither does it affect the length of labor. The incidence of fetal distress is actually reduced, he reports, for women who continue to exercise throughout their pregnancies. His studies have yet to uncover a single case of unexplained demise, fetal trauma, cord accident, or clinical utero-placenta insufficiency in the fetuses of exercising women. And women who remain active throughout their pregnancies have more than an 85 percent chance of having a normal vaginal delivery.

Clapp is particularly interested in placentas — more specifically, the growth of the placenta as a result of exercise. The placenta is a membranous organ that lines the uterine wall and helps protect and cradle the baby. Clapp believes that the largest placentas and babies have been produced due to vigorous workout

Bobsledders and Moms: Alex and Liz clown around at a German competition.

programs during the critical period of placenta growth. This theory, as Clapp explains, has been confirmed by "using ultrasoundography to estimate changes in placental volume." Simply put, Clapp believes that exercise produces larger placentas, which offer healthier, stronger wombs and, thus, healthier babies. He also believes exercise results in easier deliveries.

In fact, as Liz went into the hospital to have her baby (she was already in labor), she stopped in front of the hospital sign to pose for a picture so that her first-born, later to be named Austin, would see where he was born. Two hours later, mama and baby were fine.

Like Liz, Alex also had her (second) baby in record time. Both women firmly believe their exercise regimens made for easier deliveries. After only five pushes, Laura Katherine was born to Alex and Robb, and while the doctor sewed her up from her episiotomy, Alex was sitting up telling jokes. Her physician, Dr. Ann Wurst, would later call this the gold-medal push plan.

As encouraging as all of this is for pregnant women who wish to exercise, it is equally important for pregnant women to confer with their physicians first. Education, training, monitoring fetal development, and safety are extremely important for pregnant athletes. In fact, Clapp prefers to see a woman and discuss these issues *before* she becomes pregnant so that both doctor and patient understand what to expect. Because all patients and athletes are different, each woman may respond differently to exercise during pregnancy.

Like Clapp, Dr. Kevin Hackett points out that no matter what the level at which an athlete is performing, whether she is just beginning an exercise program or continuing intense training, understanding how her pregnancy will change her body and abilities is crucial. Low self-esteem can attack when you least expect it. And despite the glow of her pregnancy, the now-rounding woman periodically finds herself becoming depressed over her body's changes. Both Clapp and Hackett lecture on the importance of mothers-to-be having positive mental attitudes about their bodies, and their acceptance of certain physical changes during pregnancy.

Exercise is part of a positive mental attitude, and at Physicians for Women's Health, based in Columbus, Ohio, Hackett and his partners built a new practice complete with a workout facility and an exercise physiologist on-site to help patients work out safely during and after pregnancy.

Athletes seem to have an easier time adjusting to the physical changes during pregnancy and setting positive mental attitudes. Possibly because they are apt to be more in tune with their bodies and to possess a finer understanding of those changes, depression rates are lower among athletes.

Are you a mother or are you an athlete? It is a question that once, through ignorance, might have been asked. It should be no longer. Too many strong women athletes with healthy, beautiful babies have shown us the way. Too many strong athletes have proven to be better than ever *with* babies. It seems to be a pointless debate. Are you a mother or are you an athlete? As sports psychologist Coleen Hacker (who worked with the U.S. women's soccer team and mother Joy Fawcett) laughs, "That's like you asking me what time it is and me telling you the sky is blue!"

Lisa Leslie's response to those who would have her choose between modeling and basketball is appropriate for mother-athletes as well. "I'm passionate about both," she says, "and when I'm doing both, I'm giving you me. . . . The point is, I am a woman, always."[1]

Maybe doubters think once an athlete becomes a mother she can't possibly be as aggressive as she once was.

During the 1996-97 U.S. bobsled trials, Kathy Taylor was learning how to push the bobsled on the dry-land track. Taylor, a 32-year-old mother of three, is an adorable, slender athlete with good foot speed. But she was having problems adjusting to the "hit" on the sled. To look at her you just know she was a cheerleader, cute and perky, who said things like "golly" and "gee whiz."

Coach Steve Maiorca was instructing Taylor on what he thought was needed — more aggression. What he and the rest of us didn't realize was she already had the aggression; she was just working out the actual movements — thus, the hesitation. But, honestly, who expects a woman like Kathy Taylor to be really aggressive?

As Maiorca leaned over to coach Taylor, she fumed, "I just want to push the shit out of this motherf----r."

The coach's eyes lit up and several people burst out laughing.

Maiorca switched gears. "Well, okay, then, I want you to push the shit out of this thing and run the bastard all the way down!!"

She did, too.

We continue to chip away at society's stereotypes and doubts about us. Our storm winds continue to blow down discriminatory walls, opening new paths for our children, paths like the one chosen by Kelly McCormick, daughter of Pat McCormick. In 1984, the younger McCormick competed in the Olympics for the U.S., winning the silver medal in diving and, true to her mother's path, she returned to compete in the 1988 Games, earning a bronze medal. To date, they are the only Olympic mother/daughter diving team.

Perhaps there will be a mother/daughter bobsled and skeleton team one day. Already, Alex's daughter Kerri asks, "Can we go to the track? I want to exercise." Only three years old and already a runner, Kerri is the fastest child in her class (according to her teachers who can't catch her). While Alex was training for the bobsled nationals, Kerri literally grew up running the track with her mama. One day, Kerri ran four 100-meter dashes with Alex and Michelle. On the last sprint, Kerri's fists were drawn up tight, her little face pushed up toward the sky, as she ran as fast as she could to catch up with us. As we cheered her on, her pants fell down, but she kept running. With another 40 meters to go, Kerri never lost her stride. Already focused and determined, she's a champion.

The children of female athletes not only benefit from team bonding, they promote it. First Lady Hillary Clinton's book, *It Takes A Village,* is based on the African proverb, "It takes a village to raise a child." It also takes a village to support a mother-athlete. And, as we have seen time and time again, female athletes truly come together as villages to care for young ones.

We the authors have shared the wonderment of "It takes a village." When we work out at Accelerate Ohio, the trainers allow Alex's younger daughter Katie to come to the gym. Always content with her bottle and beloved "Donna" doll, she sits back and watches people running on the treadmill, lifting weights, or doing plyometrics. While Alex and Michelle work out, Katie wanders from trainer to trainer, sits in on office meetings, and even "works out" with other athletes. Welcomed and wanted, Katie has become part of the Accelerate Ohio family and part of the village.

Teams, trainers, coaches, and families repeatedly draw together to make motherhood and sports a happy combination. For Vivian Stringer, then the women's basketball coach at University of Iowa (she now coaches at Rutgers), her team voted to switch practices to 5 a.m. after Stringer's husband died, so that Stringer would be allowed to spend time with her children and still coach the team to the NCAA "sweet sixteen."

5 a.m.?

5 a.m.!

For us, the epitome of the village mentality is the story of the gold medal-winning U.S. women's soccer team. Just three weeks after having a baby girl, soccer player Joy Fawcett was planning to return to the 1994 world cup tour with her teammates. Next stop, Beijing. But as she looked at the baby formula and food, diapers, portable crib, stroller, high chair, car seat, clothing, and toys piled in the middle of her living room, she tearfully realized she could not do this alone. Then came the village.

One by one, without her asking, Fawcett's teammates called, each offering to carry a baby item. They had all limited themselves to one bag so that they could also carry a baby item. It was the beginning of an amazing relationship between then three-week-old Katlyn and the entire U.S. women's soccer team.

Fawcett told us that as Katlyn got older and was sleeping though the nights, she actually had a waiting list of teammates who wanted to sleep *with* Katlyn. They took turns playing with, watching, carrying, reading to, and sitting with the baby. As the months passed, there were times when Fawcett found herself alone in the middle of the field doing warm-ups because the rest of the team was on the sidelines watching Katlyn take her first steps, say her first words, clap her hands, or just do something cute. Fawcett would say, "You guys, you're gonna get me in trouble." But she never did get in trouble, probably because the coaches were also watching Katlyn do her "firsts."

As the 1996 Olympic Games rolled around, Katlyn was turning two years old. Much of her life on the road had been missed by her father, Michael Fawcett. During the Olympic Games, teammate Julie Foudy gave Joy Fawcett a video and asked that she watch it. "I thought, 'Okay, I'll watch it later.'" Fawcett says. "There were a lot of other things going on. I knew that Julie had been taping a lot of things — all our trips in different countries and stuff." But Foudy kept after Fawcett until she finally sat down to view the tape. What Foudy had handed Fawcett was not a tape of all their soccer experiences, but a documentary on Katlyn as she had grown up from three weeks old to two years old with her 21 aunts.

Sitting there, watching her daughter, Fawcett realized that every "first" Michael had missed, every smile or giggle, was being played before her eyes. As she repeated this story to us, we couldn't help but tear up, and we suspect Michael has rarely had a finer gift.

Now that the Olympics are over, Katlyn's life has changed dramatically. Does she miss her aunts, we wondered? After two years of sleep-overs and constant companionship, it has to be hard.

"Yesterday," Fawcett laughed, "we were driving in the car and Katlyn started doing her cheers." Not just a distraction on the sidelines, Katlyn was also a cheerleader for the U.S. women's soccer team, and every team player had made sure Katlyn knew her cheers. While Fawcett drove along their hometown streets, Katlyn suddenly broke into a cheer, "Go, Julie! Go, Julie!," "Go, go, go, Mia!," and so on.

One thing is clear: while we are all from different sports with different child care needs and demands, we all struggle with the same problems. Travel, for example, is an issue for every competitive athlete-mother. As we concluded our interview with basketball player Valerie Still, she asked Alex what she does about child care while competing on the World Cup circuit. We discussed Gwen Torrence, Michelle Rohl, Sandra Farmer-Patrick. Still was reflective: "I don't know, maybe ten years from now when the ABL is off and running, they will set up contracts that include things like nannies and day cares." Wouldn't that be something?

Are you a mother or are you an athlete?

Hmmm. We'll always be mothers. We'll always be (we hope) athletes. There is no "either." There is no "or." Still is a perfect example. While we marveled at the idea of her breastfeeding while playing full-contact, body slamming, in-your-face basketball, Still merely stated, "It's not fair to Aaron to stop nursing because of basketball." There was never a question. She does both, but she admits it has been difficult. Still's idea of nanny contracts is a good one. As women's sports grow, wouldn't it be wonderful to see major sponsors also adopt the "It takes a village" concept, writing child care into contracts?

As for the children? What a great world Katlyn and Aaron were born into, watching their mommies play sports, cheering on all their "aunts," and traveling around the world to meet other athletes. What a wonderful way to start life! Fawcett, Still, and all the other athlete-moms have made one thing very clear: one can be both an athlete and a mother. It's not always easy but, then, what is that is worth having?

Chapter Six

Journeywomen

> *It is now time for all women*
> *of colorful mind,*
> *who are aware of the cycles*
> *of night and day*
> *and the dance of the moon in her tides,*
> *to arise.*
>
> — Dhyani Ywahoo

We first learned of U.S. high jumper Louise Ritter during an ESPN segment entitled "Women of Gold." That was also the first time we had heard the term "journeyman" applied to sports. During the Seoul Games in 1984, Louise Ritter was labeled a journeyman by the media — something that in sports jargon (outside this chapter) is not considered a compliment. The term literally means someone who has successfully completed an apprenticeship in a craft or trade, a competent worker. But given to an athlete, the term refers to someone who is technically competent, but who is unable to excel, unable to win the gold medals or set new records.

Before Ritter even stepped out onto the Seoul track, many observers had written her off — so we were thrilled to watch the footage as Ritter continued to beat out her opponents, jumping to new heights and, ultimately, taking the gold.

Ritter is a living example of the position taken by David Perdue, our Tae Kwon Do black belt instructor. Perdue tells his students, "I'm not going to give you a belt; you have to take it!" Ritter took her Olympic gold and became, for us, the epitome of what the term "journeywoman" means here: someone who has been counted out, told that she is wasting her time, told that she should cut her losses and move on to something more practical (and, often, more traditional); someone who has heard all the nay-sayers, then, headed toward her goal and, through her determination, proved her worth and taken her prize.

Ritter never gave up. She couldn't believe that this was it, that this was all she had. She was unwilling to step back, to step away from competition until she had nothing left to give. Louise Ritter is a true journeywoman!

Often athletes have shared stories with us that illustrated how, when they dug down deep, they found something more to give of themselves to their sport. Like Ritter, those athletes believed in themselves. They could not be stopped by commentators who said they had already been all they could be.

One such athlete is Sandra Farmer-Patrick. Wendy Potter, president of WM Potter & Associates, an advertising and marketing firm which represents Farmer-Patrick, has this to say about the athlete: "One of the reasons she's been able to survive as an athlete is she's always looking for the next challenge. She's always moving on, getting stronger and better." Farmer-Patrick has endured so many injuries that many athletes would have retired. But Farmer-Patrick is persistent. She is a survivalist.

"It's one of the reasons I really like her," Potter says. "She rises to whatever challenges meet her. It's her mental and spiritual composure that allow her to endure." Truly a journeywoman.

Nordic ski jumper Karla Keck is a journeywoman. She has been told over and over to cut her losses, that she is wasting her time. But she refuses to quit (as most of the girls she jumped with did), literally jumping to new heights. She wants Nordic ski jumping to be an Olympic event for women — for herself and for the girls who follow her. "There is so much potential in this country for Nordic ski jumping," she says. "There's a 12-year-old girl, Lindsey Van, who jumped off the 120-meter (platform). I don't know any boys doing that.

"But I'm terrified for the young girls; there's nowhere for them to go. They can't stay at the OTC [Olympic training center in Lake Placid, New York]; they can't train year-round like the boys; they don't have coaches." That's why Keck is petitioning the USOC, trying to have housing and coaches and training facilities provided for the girls as well as the boys.

And the women of the ABL and WNBA are journeywomen. Particularly the players in the ABL, which does not have the huge support from the NBA, network television, and major commercial sponsors that the WNBA has. These women continued to play basketball, to press for a women's professional league, despite the nay-sayers. While these determined women vary greatly in size, backgrounds, personalities, they all became blurry visions in our minds. Believe it or not, this is meant as a compliment. As we went over notes and compared stories, one thing was clear: we were dealing with a group of happy, outgoing, enthusiastic, caring women who truly want to see their sport grow for the sake of little girls following in their footsteps. Across the board, all answered that children are our most valuable asset. We were swept over by their huge smiles, easy manners, and hearty handshakes. The Columbus Quest, the Philadelphia Rage, the San Jose Lasers. . . all these women were so eager to talk not about themselves, but about what this sport, what this league can do for little girls *and boys* everywhere. (We were tickled recently to see a teenage boy wearing an ABL "Little Girls Can Dream" t-shirt. Oh, yeah!)

The women of the newer WNBA (sister to the NBA) have the same reputation. While many of the overpaid stars of the NBA are known to slight their fans, dodging autograph seekers and even eye contact, the women are just the opposite. Take Teresa Weatherspoon of the New York Liberty, for example. She spies a little girl wearing her number 11 jersey. "Hey, baby! You my girl! You got my shirt!" While children and adults line up for autographs, Weatherspoon practically accosts her fans. She kisses one little girl and tells her, "Be sweet, tweety bird!" The flustered child can only utter, "Oh, my God!" Can anyone imagine Charles Barkley doing this?

Weatherspoon, like all the women basketball players, is reflective about her new station in life. It is not just an athletic opportunity or a job. It is the beginning of something much bigger. It is the beginning of all little girls being able to dream and fulfill those dreams. And she is part of helping those dreams become reality.

There are plenty of stories of individual journeywomen in both leagues. Andrea Lloyd of the ABL, said to be the Larry Bird of women's basketball, returned to the game only a month after knee surgery; Valerie Still continued to play after a devastating car accident and seven months after having a baby; Venus Lacey defied medical prognoses and is able to play because she never gave up the dream to run and play.

Although Taj McWilliams of the ABL's Philadelphia Rage, is 6'3" and was a high school basketball star, she did not play for an NCAA school. University of Georgia recruited her, but the coach wouldn't allow McWilliam's daughter to stay with her. Her father and high school coach told her she had blown her big chance by getting pregnant her senior year of high school. "You could have been a great basketball player," they told her. But she never gave up and now she is living her dream. She also works in a home for runaway girls, who are at risk to be teenage moms, counseling them. She believes one of her missions is to reach out to young girls.

Whether a basketball fan or not, it is hard not to be enchanted with the way these players have dedicated themselves not only to their sport, but also to their communities.

"It's just great to see the kids benefit," says Sonja Tate of the Quest.

"Are we pioneers?" asks Trisha Stafford of the San Jose Lasers. "We're founders of this league (the ABL), but we're not the pioneers. True pioneers set the stage, like Cheryl Miller, when it wasn't written about or talked about."

As though there had been a requirement of poise, graciousness, and journeywoman-ism for induction into the leagues, these women have set a new standard for athletics. And for what they want. As the Reebok commercial presents it, these women truly are saying:

> "We are not waiting for approval or permission, and we are definitely not waiting for anyone to let us play. We're not waiting for anything — except the ball. This is our time. This is our league!"

We wouldn't have it any other way.

Their passion for their sport is infectious. It reminded us of trainer-to-the-stars Radu's passion for fitness. We immediately understood why so many big names go to him. The passion that he expressed to us was unmatched by anyone else we interviewed. This man definitely is a believer in determination and will, a belief he passes on to his clients. Later, we laughed as we reviewed Alex's notes because as Radu began yelling, Alex's handwriting got bigger and bigger.

The interview started out quietly enough. Radu shared with us his concern about the lack of understanding Americans have about the importance of physical education. "Sensing the direction of energy, making concise decisions, and acting upon them," Radu said, "are all sharpened from sport."

When Radu himself turned the subject to "positive attitudes," we asked him if he had seen a shirt a lot of kids wear today. It reads in large letters: "Second Sucks."

"What?" his voice rose.

We guessed that he had not seen the shirt before, but he had a reaction and he made his views clear. "Once the creator of the Olympics said this, and I quote, 'The most important thing in the Olympic Games is not to win but to take part, just as the most important thing in life is not the triumph but the struggle. The essential thing is not to have conquered but to have fought well!' To say that second sucks, it is very bad. We should not even discuss this. I think. . . I think the man who created that shirt should be shot! You cannot always win, but does this mean it was not worthwhile? Look at the Muhammed Ali-Joe Frazier fight. Someone had to lose, but it was spectacular. Always, we will remember that fight, the courage they showed."

Florence Griffith Joyner has said she lost many more races

than she ever won. She will be remembered for her victories, but losing was part of her growth. Who would tell Flo Jo she sucks?

During the 1994 Lillehammer Games, speedskater Bonnie Blair missed winning the bronze medal in the 1500-meter relay by three-one-hundredths of a second. She had already won gold in the 500 and 1000 meters, becoming the first American woman to win five gold medals in Olympic history, the first American to win a gold medal in the same Winter event in three Olympic Games, and the most decorated U.S. athlete in Winter Olympic history. "The media and everybody got carried away with the medals I won," she says, "but what I remember most was the time I got for the 1500 was my personal best." Blair tries to achieve her personal best in daily life. Who's going to tell Blair she sucks for just missing the bronze?

Before the 1992 Barcelona Games, Shannon Miller watched quietly from the sidelines as everyone predicted glory for world champion Kim Zmeskal. Miller went on to win two silver and three bronze medals at the Games and then two world championships, and become this country's most decorated gymnast. Before the 1996 Atlanta Games, Miller again watched quietly all the hoopla about teammate Dominique Moceanu, then went on to lead the team to a team gold (the first for an American gymnastics team) and to win an individual gold on the balance beam. Miller did not let publicity (or lack thereof) or injuries or age sway her from her goal of an Olympic gold medal. Who's going to tell Miller she sucks for winning silver in Barcelona?

Ironman athlete Julie Moss gained fame in 1982 when she collapsed while leading the Ironman Triathlon World Championship with just a few hundred yards to the finish line. ABC's Wide World of Sports captured the heart-wrenching moment on film, as Moss crawled to the finish line, being passed by Kathleen McCartney with just yards to go. But her heroics resulted in an explosion of triathlon participation. "Julie Moss gave the world the definition 'Ironman Spirit' in 1982; she set out to finish what she started and she persevered until she reached the finish line," says David Yates, president of the World Triathlon Corporation. Who's going to tell Julie Moss that she sucks?

Radu was still chewing on the t-shirt business.

"I hate this 'second sucks.'" We played it safe and did not mention that No Fear has a t-shirt that reads: "If you can't win, don't play!"

Radu continued: "Perhaps you are on a team that works very hard, you train hard together, but just because you work together, another team might work a little better. Teams are like watches. Every piece is vital to the watch, each piece has its function, just like the team. There are leaders, supporters, followers. Maybe you lose one time because the other team has one better part, but it does not mean you suck! I do not like this shirt!"

Radu is not the only one who feels this way. In fact, most serious athletes do not buy into the philosophy that winning is all that counts. Take swimmer Danielle Lundy, for example. At 11 years of age, she is a three-time Pennsylvania state champion in breast stroke. In 1994, 1995, and 1996, she was ranked number one in the nation for her age group.

We learned from Lundy that one of her favorite athletes (besides Amanda Beard and Jackie Joyner-Kersee) is Summer Sanders. When asked how she felt when Sanders failed to qualify for the 1996 Atlanta Games, Lundy responded, "I felt really bad for her, but I'm not going to say she failed. She didn't achieve what she wanted to achieve, but she didn't fail. People don't fail when they try." (In fact, Sanders was hired by NBC as a commentator.) How many 11-year-olds have that kind of perspective? Yet this 11-year-old girl already gracefully embodies the code of the Olympics.

U.S. softball player Lisa Fernandez was told by a coach at the tender age of 12 that she would never be a champion pitcher because her arms were too short. "He said I wouldn't be able to really compete past the age of 16," Fernandez says.[1] For Fernandez, softball was her life. This could have been potentially devastating news, but Fernandez did not let it be so. With the journeywoman spirit, Fernandez continued her training and dreaming.

Then, at the 1995 Pan American Games qualifier tournament, the 24-year-old Fernandez devastated the competition by pitching a no-hitter, enabling the U.S. to win the gold medal.

Swimmer Angel Martino was banned from the 1988 Olympics after her birth control pills caused her to test positive in a controversial drug test (a testing method which is no longer used, because it is so unreliable). "I did get to two more Olympics, but it was really hard" to get past the 1988 ban. "I took a year off; I quit! I just couldn't do it. I thought, 'Why am I doing this?' But after a while, I realized this was my dream, so why should I let someone take it from me?"

She didn't, swimming to one gold and one bronze in the 1992 Barcelona Games and two golds and two bronze medals in the 1996 Atlanta Games. And while she never received a formal apology about the ban, she says many people have privately apologized to her, telling her, "We know you didn't do anything wrong."

By the early 1980s, Mary Decker Slaney had become the best female runner in the world in the mile, the 5,000 meters, and the 10,000 meters. But a combination of bad luck and injuries have kept her from an Olympic medal although she has made four Olympic teams. She has undergone at least 20 operations on her legs, endured the U.S. boycott of the 1980 Moscow Olympics, and been injured (accidentally) by a fellow competitor. Tests following the Atlanta Games where she had failed to reach the 5,000-meter final revealed she has exercise-induced asthma.

Finally, properly medicated, she was running like her old self, winning the most recent Millrose Games handily. But just as she had begun talking about competing in the Sydney Olympics — at the age of 42 — she was hit with her newest, and perhaps toughest, challenge. She was banned from competition by USA Track and Field and the International Amateur Athletic Federation (IAAF) because of a drug test during the Olympic trials which showed high ratios of the male sex hormone testosterone. The problem is this test has been shown to be highly unreliable for women, since menstruation, birth control pills, alcohol, and bacteria in the urine can affect its outcome. Slaney has tested clean for drugs for 24 years. Since the Olympic trials, she has been tested six times and all six tests were negative. She has now been cleared by USA Track and Field, but not before she lost most of the 1997 season. And she is still awaiting a decision by the IAAF.

Still she refuses to quit; she continues her fight to run. "People I run against no longer tell me they had my poster on their wall," she says. "Now they thank me for showing they have 10 more years of running."[2]

Even athletes who would never have been considered journeywomen — women like Bonnie Blair, who was never counted out — struggled with their own very private accomplishments. While we all only saw her great speedskating triumphs, we never thought of everyday workouts as something she wrestled with. But for Blair, loop training was a challenge. While training, she and her teammates would run up a hill, on a straight, down a hill, on a straight, and start all over again. Blair did ten loops to the guys' twelve. Her goal was to finish before the men finished their twelfth loop. "I was ahead of them on the hill. I could call it ahead because I was so far behind." While the guys focused on Blair, trying to pass her, Blair was determined to finish her set before they finished theirs. Unlike Fernandez or Ritter, this great feat was not performed before millions of spectators. In fact, few might even consider this a feat, but to Blair this determination carried over into her races, giving her that extra push.

Bonnie Blair

Few also would consider super-model Cindy Crawford or singer/actress Vanessa Williams athletes, but Crawford proved something to herself she never imagined she could do. And she did it, of course, through sport and the journeywoman's perseverance.

Crawford was headed for the big screen, landing a part in the film *Fair Game* with William Baldwin. It was her big break. Together, Radu and Crawford looked over the script. It called for her character to run desperately, jump onto a moving train, and punch out a bad guy. When Radu approached the stunt coordinator on the set about Crawford's training he was told, "Just keep her strong and toned. Don't worry about it."

The stunt coordinators and director were not even considering having Crawford do any of her own stunts. In truth, it had not occurred to anyone she could. Besides, they didn't want her getting hurt. Radu had other plans. While he didn't intend for her to actually make the jump onto the train, he did want the scenes to look as real as possible. Crawford trained as though she really were punching someone out, as though she were running for her life, and as though she were trying to jump on a moving train. In reality, all Crawford was expected to do was the lead-up to the stunts.

Finally, the time for the big scene came. Crawford was supposed to run hard to a certain point alongside the train, then drop off. A stunt double would take her place to catch the train. Crawford would later tell Radu, as she was running along she realized that all her training with him in preparation for that very scene had actually been a lot more difficult than the actual stunt.

Imagine then the fallen expressions, the gaping mouths, and pounding hearts of the entire film crew when Crawford did not stop at her mark. As the train roared on by so, too, did Crawford. The cameras kept rolling as Crawford strained, dug down deep and chased that train, jumping on at the last moment, making a spectacular stunt for the movie.

Radu praises Crawford, saying, "I had given her the tools to achieve, and she used those tools to accomplish more than was expected of her, and more than she expected of herself."

Like Crawford, another one of Radu's clients was headed for the big screen in *Eraser* with Arnold Schwarzenegger. Vanessa

Williams initially went to Radu for her casting as *Spider Woman*, and found herself climbing the thick rope that hangs from Radu's gym ceiling. Hers was the same story as Crawford's: Williams only needed to look good. Very rapidly, though, the training carried over into new challenges, causing her to push herself beyond her own limits. "That seed I put in her built her confidence to new heights," Radu says of Williams. "There is nothing she can't do now. Her discovery of her own strength has empowered her. I wish all people could learn the feeling of such triumph. She may not go 600 miles per hour like bobsledding, but she can go 60 miles per hour!"

And what about bobsledding? It's true, we like to think of ourselves as journeywomen and many of the women we have met in bobsledding (Canadians, Brits, Swiss, Germans, and Latvians) share our feelings. We have all been told that this isn't a sport for women, that we're too small, too old. . . . You name it, we've heard it. We were counted out almost before we began, but we have refused to go away — despite the lumps. And there have been many.

While the men have teams of athletes who have been driving for more than a decade, the women's teams are fairly new. After all, bobsledding is a kamikaze sport that does not appeal to most women. Every year we have new, fresh-faced enthusiasts who slide from the mile once, crash, and never return. So each year we train new drivers and each year there are crashes. It is part of the sport.

In the early 1996 season, Liz, riding as a brakewoman, went speeding out of control through the turns called "Zig Zag" in Lake Placid, New York. For experienced bobsledders, "out of control through Zig Zag" evokes an instant response of shudders. One of the track workers told us that as the sled tore through the finish curve Liz looked like a rag doll, flopping outside the sled. "She looked like she was dead," he said solemnly. When at last the sled stopped, Liz had suffered a torn rotary cuff in her shoulder, a grade-two concussion, two broken ribs, damaged wrists and lower back, and major bodily bruises.

When we helped carry her into the ambulance, she was fighting back the tears. "Dammit," she said, "I just wanted one good trip." No one woman epitomizes the struggles of the U.S. women's bobsled team better than Liz Parr-Smestad. She has suffered more crashes than anyone, acting as various drivers' brakewoman and as a beginning driver. But she is relentless. She won't go away because she knows the potential is there. She truly wants to see the women's team succeed and, moreover, she wants a piece of that pie. She's earned it. (It is ironic that she also is a mother, and one of the women told to decide between motherhood and athletics.)

When the authors made the first women's bobsled team, we thought we would run, push the sled, hop in the back, and go for that exhilarating ride. Of course, we soon learned there was much more. We had to learn to walk the track before a run; to visualize our runs; how to handle the turns, the speed, the pressure; how to sit; how to always look six feet ahead while driving; how to crash. And much of this we had to learn on our own. Laurie Millett, one of the first four American women to compete internationally, climbed into the back of a bobsled behind Michelle in Calgary, Alberta, although Michelle had never actually touched a bobsled before. She climbed in behind Michelle again in St. Moritz, Switzerland (one of the most difficult tracks in the world), although they only had about 10 hours ice time, so they could compete in the first international race including American women.

Persistence is the hallmark of the journeywoman. And there is not much glamour at this stage in one's career. Take the brake position in a bobsled. The brakewoman, crouched over in the back of the sled, holding on to the side bars, head down, counting out the turns in her mind, is part of the sled and track. Sitting just inches above the ice in a cold steel sled, there is no cushioning to pad against "tags" on the walls. (A "tag" is the understated way we describe how our bodies are slammed against the icy wall and only our required kidney belts can help hold our organs in place.)

The brakewoman can hear the blades (runners) cutting the ice, hear the rattle of the heavy sled, feel the turns. Then, just before there is a crash, there is the worst sound imaginable in the sport of bobsledding — momentary silence. (The sound we bobsledders love to hear is that of the announcer saying, "Through and down," meaning the race is completed and the team finished the mountain on its blades. We like to hear "through and down!" very much.)

The silence means the blades have left the ice.

Then, *CRASH*!

Airborne only briefly, the sound that follows — directly after the driver and brakewoman mutter "oh, shiiiiit!" — is that of the sled coming down hard on the ice. In place of the sweet sound of blades cutting ice, there are several new sounds. The capsized sled crashes through each turn, tearing at the sled, and ripping the brakewoman from her seat. While the driver is usually (luckily) under the cowling, worried sick about her teammate, the brakewoman is left to fight it out with the mountain.

The U.S. Women's Bobsledding Team in Calgary. From left to right: top row, Krista Ford; second row, Jean Racine, Michelle Powe, Chrissy Spiezio and Alex Powe-Allred; third row, Elena Primerano, Sue Blazejewski and Meg Henderson; in front, Jill Bakken.

The pull of gravity is tremendous. On her sides, the brakewoman hangs on for dear life. It feels as though two very large hands are prying her fingers off the side bars. Then there is the sound of her helmet grinding against the ice. It is a constant "ssccchhhhh" sound that never lets up, except when the sled follows a new curve, sliding to the opposite wall. For a brief moment, sled and woman are separated from the ice wall. There is a moment to catch her breath before the sled leaves that turn and crashes again against the opposite wall. Shoulders are on fire from the ice burn that occurs to any part of the body that is hanging out of the careening sled.

Gritting her teeth and pushing against the ice with her head as the sled races down the mountain at 60, 70, 80 miles per hour, the brakewoman fights the track – a useless effort – with neck strength in an effort to save her shoulder from more ice burn or worse.

The only other sound one is aware of is the grunting, the sound of exhaustion and pain while waiting for the ride from hell to end. And finally, as the sled travels through the finish curve and slows to a stop, silence falls again. Then the brakewoman can fall in a heap, listening to her own breath.

"Oh, thank God. It's over."

There is rustling in the front of the sled and the worried driver begins to stir, trying to find her way out of the ropes. Her voice is muffled through her helmet. "You okay?" she calls out, still not really seeing her brakewoman.

"Thank God it's over," the brake will say. Footsteps approach, paramedics check the sled's passengers, and then track workers flip the sled upright again. A track coach will ask, "You okay?" and we will nod.

Then we go back to the top and try again. We have to because we have to get it right. We have to prove to the FIBT (the international federation for bobsled) and IOC (the International Olympic Committee) that we are competent, qualified drivers and brakes, and the only way that's going to happen is to go over and over again.

During the 1995-96 season the women's team of eight took their lumps. The total damage was a broken collarbone; two broken ribs; a broken foot; four grade-two concussions; an emergency root canal; an injured sternum; torn ligaments and cartilage; a torn rotary cuff; a broken hand; numerous back, head, shoulder, and leg injuries; a knee surgery; and countless bruises.

In fact, these were not just "concussions," our women suffered. They were mind-scrambling blows that scared other teammates.

Two examples we now giggle about. After having "cracked her coconut" coming out of Zig Zag (one of the most treacherous curves in the world) in 1996, Chrissy was asked by an emergency attendant to name the president of United States. Long pause. She looked expectantly at Alex, her faithful brakewoman, the woman who stood by and protected her at all times.

"I'm not going to tell you!" Alex loudly protested. Alex knew that Chrissy would try to pretend she was okay. Forced to answer, Chrissy guessed George Bush. Sorry. Wrong guy, wrong party, wrong year.

"Take her away, boys," Alex said.

Only weeks before, Michelle and Liz had crashed on the track in Winterberg, Germany. Michelle was knocked unconscious and suffered a concussion and broken collarbone. When she came to, she was asked by the paramedics if she knew where she was. She looked at her worried brakewoman. Like Alex, this was one time Liz was going to let Michelle fly solo. Michelle said, "Wellll, everyone's speaking German, so. . . Germany?"

"Nehmen Sie sie Hinweg, Jungen," Liz sighed. (Loosely translated: "Take her away, boys.")

This is our sport. It's about training, lifting weights, pushing a bob. It is about guts, nerve, knowing when to walk away, suck it up, blow it off. It's about friendship, teamwork, and companionship. It's about static strength and power. It's about courage, crashing, hoping, praying, believing, and celebrating. For now, for us, it is also about refusing to be counted out, about embarking on a journey in which we may never see the pay-offs personally, but a journey that should help our daughters to progress and to flourish.

Chapter Seven

Bumper Stickers in Times Square

You intend no doubt
to give me nothing,
and are not aware
the gift has already been
received. . .
For I am rich;
no cheap and ragged
beggar
but a queen. . .

— Alice Walker, "Gift,"
Revolutionary Petunias & Other Poems

In 1994, in response to a directive by the United States Olympic Committee (USOC) that each federation must have at least 10 percent representation of its minority sex, the U.S. Bobsled Federation held try-outs for the first U.S. women's bobsled team in history. Eight women made that team.

Here we were: the first female bobsledders. We were on our way.

But on our way where? To what? We had no money, no traveling coach, no sleds, no idea what we were doing. Money was (and is) scarce, and all of the incoming money was earmarked for the men's team. Initially, the big question was how to raise money?

To be clear, the entire fund-raising issue is frustrating and complicated for USOC-sanctioned teams, i.e., all sports for both genders. In the case of the U.S. Bobsled and Skeleton Federation, it is chronically underfunded. Naturally, competition within the federation for scarce bucks created tensions, and the outcome for the women's team was trying. We were told we must raise our own money, but we must not approach sponsors already supporting the men's team. And we must not approach sponsors *not* supporting the men's team because those sponsors were being courted by the men's team.

So, now what? Well, suggested a federation board member, how about having a bake sale?

A bake sale? To raise money for four $10,000 sleds, not to mention gear for eight women, and a coach's salary. That's a lot of flour! But this wasn't the only helpful advice we received from well-meaning, if condescending, observers.

Perhaps, another federation official suggested, we could each go to New York City (four of us would have to buy airline tickets to get there), and peddle bumper stickers in Times Square. We had just been discussing how we could raise money in an efficient manner. Somehow this was not the image we were after. Nevermind the costs of vendors' licenses, airline tickets, hotel rooms and board. We did, however, go on to have clever bumper stickers produced. (And for a mere $4, you too can be the proud owner of bumper stickers that read either *"I Brake for Bobsledders! U.S. Women's Bobsled Team"* or *"Woman Driver and Proud of It! U.S. Women's Bobsled Team."* Money raised supports the women's team. Just write to the American Women's Bobsled and Skeleton Association, 117 La Salle Dr., Yonkers, NY 10710, for your bumper stickers.)

Adversity lies in the path of all female athletes to some degree. What if Babe Didrikson-Zaharias or Wilma Rudolph or Jackie Joyner-Kersee had listened to the nay-sayers? Or Mary

Lou Retton, who became the first American gymnast ever to win gold in the individual all-around and score a perfect "10" on the vault? "I'm a very positive person," Retton says. "If I'm in a group and there's a nay-sayer, I leave the group because I don't want that person bringing me down." Attitude is everything.

What if the Women's Sports Foundation executive director Donna Lopiano had listened to the nay-sayers? Lopiano participated in 26 national championships in four sports and was a nine-time All-American in softball, a sport in which she played on six national championship teams. She is a member of the National Sports Hall of Fame, the National Softball Hall of Fame, and the Texas Women's Hall of Fame. She has coached college men's and women's volleyball, and women's basketball, field hockey, and softball. And she is currently #41 on *The Sporting News'* list of "The 100 Most Influential People in Sports." Talk about determination.

So — with visions of future Olympics dancing in our heads — we have prevailed at each new roadblock, and a few of us have become even more determined than before.

However determined, the basic problem remained — how to raise funds, without which our program would die. For the first two years, most of us supported ourselves — often aided by our families — in the most expensive sport in the Winter Olympics, and most of us put ourselves in fairly serious debt doing it. In the 1995-96 season, some sponsorship was found for new personal gear for the women's team and to pay some travel costs for *one* of the four two-person teams. But everyone else was on her own for the travel, training, and other expenses. Individually, we each managed to find some help from interested individuals and companies. For instance, Powerbar and AirTouch

Cellular have helped Alex and Michelle. Limited Edition of San Francisco provided 12 flag jackets for the first women's bobsled team, and these jackets were our only team uniform for two years. Fund-rasier Earl Ashton (of Merrill Lynch) bought parkas, snowpants, gloves, and spandex uniforms for the women in 1995.

Then, in 1996, one financial sponsor —American Skandia Life Assurance Corporation — finally found us as a team. Although the money committed by American Skandia is not enough to support all eight women on the team, it is a great start, and American Skandia has committed support through the 2002 Games! Unfortunately, contrary to what we had earlier understood, women's bobsledding very likely will not be included in the 2002 Games. The U.S. representative to the IOC, Anita DeFrantz, confirmed to us in late 1997 that women's bobsled "is not on the 2002 program." So we look to 2006. We continue to plug ahead, and the women who are not supported continue to support themselves or look for outside sponsorship; they continue to learn how to promote themselves.

The problem of lack of support is not unique to the bobsled team or other national women's teams or *any* female athletes. Female athletes at all levels have felt the cold shoulders of coaches, media, and the public. For example, although more than two million girls participate in high school sports (one in three) and 110,000 women play on NCAA teams, females account for fewer than five percent of all sports stories (print or broadcast). In fact, until the 1990s, newspaper sports pages dedicated more column space to horses and dogs than to female athletes.

In the 52 weeks between February 1993 and February 1994, women were awarded the cover of *Sports Illustrated* six times. The first was a model for the infamous swimsuit edition, the second was Monica Seles with a knife in her back, and three and four were the widows of baseball players. Number five was tennis star Mary Pierce, who was being stalked by her allegedly abusive father. And six was Nancy Kerrigan after she was clubbed in the knee.

The statistics are not much better for females outside athletics: only 15 percent of references on the front pages of newspapers are references to women (who make up 52 percent of the U.S. population and own about a third of the nation's companies). Patricia Ireland, president of the National Organization for Women, protests that women today are powerful, strong, and beautiful, but "you wouldn't know that when the only three women who appeared on the covers of major newsmagazines (in 1995) were Claudia Schiffer, Susan Smith, and Princess Di." A supermodel, a child killer, and a princess?

What about women like Carol Bellamy, the executive director of UNICEF; or Nanci "The Fabulous Sports Babe" Donnellan, the shock jock of the radio waves and ESPN2; or Cris Dolan, dare-devil athlete and ABC Multimedia Group executive?

It's not surprising that sponsors and the viewing public do not always take female athletes seriously. After all, media executives don't. Case-in-point: one ex-ESPN executive told us that his advice to a daughter in sports would be just to have fun. "You'll never be a professional," he'd tell her, "so just have fun. Don't put up with the bullshit, and only fight battles you can win."

You'll never be a professional? But what about Rachael Myllymaki who, by the age of 18, had pocketed over $250,000 in earnings from rodeo racing? As a five-time professional rodeo circuit champion, it cannot be argued that Myllymaki is anything but a professional athlete. At the tender age of 13, she won the Dodge National Circuit Rodeo, netting $8,500 in just three days work. Thirteen years old!

What about professional tennis players like Monica Seles and Steffi Graf? Or figure skaters like Kristi Yamaguchi and Nancy Kerrigan? What about the new women's professional basketball leagues? Watch those women play just one game and no one would question the dedication, athleticism, or professionalism of their game. And when we spoke to agent David Bober to try to set up an interview with Mia Hamm, we learned that Hamm was in Los Angeles filming a Pert Plus shampoo commercial. Both Sheryl Swoopes and Monica Seles have their own signature shoe lines, as does skier Picabo Street; commentator Robin Roberts is one of the busiest women in the business, and Bonnie Blair, Janet Evans and Mary Ellen Clark are on motivational speaking circuits. And everyone wants a piece of the Sports Babe.

It was no surprise, then, when we asked all the super athletes, authors, commentators, and celebrities about the executive's "you'll never be a professional" theory, that their overwhelming responses were, "Huh?" "Who is this guy?" "What is he talking about?"

They did, however, agree with the "just have fun" part. As Trisha Stafford of the San Jose Lasers basketball team puts it, "Something you do daily shouldn't be a battle. You need to have fun. That's my new motto." And before Olympic race walking coach Mike DeWitt sends his athletes out, he always calls out, "Hey, have fun." As he explains, "Because if you aren't having fun, why would you be doing it? But it is hard work as well. It should be fun and it should be hard."

American Gladiator Siren says: "Of course, you don't want your daughter to take sports so seriously that she kills herself if she doesn't win, but come on! Don't let her down by telling her it's all for fun! It should be hard! The best lessons are learned from hard confrontations and making mistakes. It builds a lot of character. Only fighting a battle you can win won't teach you anything — except maybe to settle for less. What a cowardly attitude."

Whatever the intentions of the nay-sayers (and we believed the ESPN exec's intentions to be good), the result is the same: to dismiss the efforts of women in sports. After all, it's hard to believe in yourself when others don't. It's hard to keep the faith, to keep the drive alive. Which is why girls and women in these situations so often quit. For this reason alone, we need to encourage and support female athletes as much as possible. We need to take Bonnie Blair's advice and call our media more often, report stories and games, and talk about individual athletes striving for important goals. We cannot sit back and wait for the reporters to come to us. The need to get positive female role models in the forefront is imperative, just as it is important to push women's athletics to the front pages.

Nancy Woodhull was impressed with the determination and will of the female athlete. "What I find surprising," she said, "is that so many young women have female athletic role models when so few newspapers and television newscasts offer consistent coverage of women's sports. That's further evidence, to me, that women have found alternative sources of information, outside the normal media, for information that they are passionate about. Marketeers and media executives should be very wary."

Women's sports keep growing regardless of coverage, Woodhull said. And while female athletes are still sorely overlooked in most media, a new trend has begun. One that we like very much. To name only a few examples, newspapers like *The Cleveland Plain Dealer*, *The Salt Lake City Tribune*, and *The Atlanta Journal & Constitution* are innovative, following the growth of women's sports. Action photos in full color are not an unusual sight on their front pages. Scholastic sports are beginning to be covered in proportion to fan interest and participation. "A big women's game or an upset will actually push major league sports off the front page," according to Woodhull.

On January 28, 1997, the entire sports section of *The Columbus Dispatch* was about women. We were thrilled to see story after story about athletes who just happened to be female. And on February 26, 1997, Valerie Still was on the front page of the paper, swarmed by fans, because the Columbus Quest had made the ABL playoffs. Still was pictured with her arm around a small boy, leaning over him like a great athlete-role model. *Sports Illustrated* also is finally beginning to give women's sports more of the coverage they deserve.

Yet the problem for females generally remains how to promote themselves. Keeping an eye on the prize becomes difficult and confusing. The female trying to climb the ladder of success (whether in the corporate world or the sports world) must be part-businesswoman, part-public relations agent. This dual-role is particularly taxing for the amateur female athlete who, instead of concentrating on her "job" of full-time physical and mental training, must take valuable time out to promote herself and try to win the sponsorship critical for all amateur athletes. Of course, this business/PR role is not limited to women: we have seen some of our bobsledding brothers struggling for individual sponsors, too. But the problem is certainly more prevalent in women's athletics. And the barriers sturdier.

To raise public awareness and support for female athletes (professional, Olympic, college, and high school), former diver Micki King founded the Women's Sports Foundation (WSF), along with tennis great Billie Jean King (no relation) and gold medalist swimmer Donna de Varona. WSF Executive Director Donna Lopiano expresses the feelings that drove the foundation's organizers: "What would be the reaction if there were no women on MTV? If there were no women in ballet, no women on Broadway, no women in the movie industry? You'd hear people saying, 'My God, this is terrible.' Well, my God, this was terrible. Women have been kept out of a lucrative career area by being kept out of sports." The function of WSF is to promote and enhance female sports, and to act as an educational and advocacy organization for and about female athletics.

According to Micki King, the biggest promotional problem among female athletes is ignorance. Girls and women do not know how to market themselves; they still don't know the rules for getting noticed and, thereby, supported. And King should know about lack of support.

In 1960, she was 16 years old and searching for money to support her Olympic training, pool memberships, travel, and competition fees. Her father was a GM factory line worker, and from his limited income paid for everything. King approached her local paper, but "they wouldn't give me the time of day," she says. In high school, she was "allowed" to train in the school pool as long as she didn't get in the way of the boys who were training. She was not allowed to compete, however, and not allowed to earn the high school letter she coveted. She continued to train — on her own — through college, although with no help from the University of Michigan. In fact, there was no women's team because, officially, it was

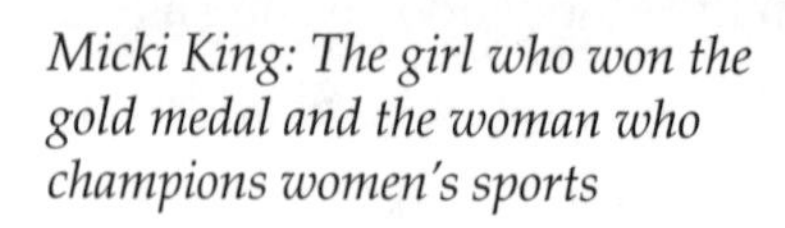

Micki King: The girl who won the gold medal and the woman who champions women's sports

"illegal" for women to dive at the University of Michigan. Because the men's diving coach liked her and saw the potential of greatness in her, he allowed her to train "unofficially" when the men did.

After King won her Olympic gold medal, the previously-uninterested and unsupportive hometown newspaper sponsored a parade for her with "Welcome Home, Micki King" banners everywhere. "I didn't know that they knew I was gone," she says. "Where were they when I really needed them?" Her high school awarded her a varsity letter. And the university, "claimed me as its own," she says. "I wondered, its own what?"

Only after she had obtained the unobtainable — an Olympic gold medal — did people take notice. But by then she (and her family) had already fought and won her battles alone. She had struggled — without public notice or interest — for money, for training facilities, for coaching, and had somehow prevailed. But female athletes (like male athletes) need sponsorship and support long before the actual Games: they need training time, facilities, coaching, sponsorship. And if that involves conducting themselves in the confident and assertive way Babe Didrikson-Zaharias did, so be it.

Didrikson-Zaharias understood the value of publicity in gaining the support she needed and she became a great self-promoter, often making predictions to the press before her meets. Her campaign began in the early 1930s when she wrote to a reporter, telling him about herself: "They said I was the athlete they have been waiting for," and "They've never seen an athlete like me before." It was not unusual for her to report to the press how well she had competed and conclude her letters by saying, "Thanks for a heading." And, as always, she got it. Because of her exuberant, flamboyant, show-off style, and her great athleticism, she captured headlines.

Only when girls and women take opportunities to succeed will society see what they can really accomplish. And only then will society truly believe in female ability and stop requiring constant, case-by-case proof.

We can all help the girls and women in our towns realize their athletic dreams. To help us help, the Women's Sports Foundation has developed a nine-point guideline on how to make girls' sports a priority in every community:

1. Form an awards and grant committee.
2. Decide which awards programs best fit your community. The Foundation (1-800-227-3988) has programs in 15 categories providing grant money for communities to distribute. They range from spirit and courage awards to various player- or woman-of-the-year awards, plus awards for adults who do the most to encourage girls to take part in sports.
3. Determine which local and national grants programs your community would like to administer. Some of these programs are funded by major corporations. Sudafed, for instance, has a national travel and training fund; young athletes can receive up to $1,500.
4. Convene a committee meeting upon receipt of awards and grants materials.
5. Distribute award nomination forms and grant application forms to school, youth and adult sport clubs, and community agencies that conduct fitness programs for girls and women (such as YMCA, Special Olympics, and Girls, Inc.).
6. Collect nominations and applications prior to the deadline.

7. Select the recipients. Multiple awards can be given to ensure diversity, but it's important that selections are made with care so that the committee, the community, and the kids all feel good about who is chosen.
8. Announce the winners at a public ceremony that the media can cover.
9. Complete a report to the Foundation about the success of your awards and grants program. The Foundation then can track how its funds are being used, perhaps decide to throw in more money if its funds were used well, and offer suggestions to make the program even better. That's what the Foundation is there for: to help educate communities and help the moms and dads who make these programs possible.

And Bonnie Blair says, don't be afraid to pick up the phone and brag about someone else. Sure, only a tiny percentage of sports sections in newspapers and sports magazines feature women on the covers, but what if they were bombarded with great stories all the time? When Blair retired, the general feeling among the press was that with both Blair and Dan Jansen gone, so was the fire for the U.S. speedskating clubs. When Blair saw two skaters win Nationals and receive no coverage, she picked up the phone and chewed out some reporters. (Well, chewed out as much as Bonnie Blair can chew someone out.) "I said, 'Look, you have a chance to really pick up the interest in speedskating. . . .'"

Female athletes and women in all other walks of life will have to continue speaking out and demonstrating extraordinary accomplishments in order to be acknowledged, in order to spark interest. What female athletes and non-athletes alike desire is simple: the same opportunities for advancement and promotion that men have, the same benefits, the same responsibilities. Such simple wishes still face resistance. Resistance which can only be beaten down by educational efforts to raise public awareness.

Demonstrating the need for continual education and awareness-building: organizers of the Australian Open tennis tournament announced in 1996 that they would discontinue the practice of presenting equal purses (prize money) for men and women. "The decision was made on the basis of what is best for the tournament," said Geoff Pollard, president of Tennis Australia. The decision increased the total prize money for the men by 17 percent, and for the women by only six percent[1], although the U.S. Tennis Association told us that in 1995 the difference in attendance between the men and women's matches was marginal.

At Wimbledon in 1996, the men's singles winner earned $628,000, while the women's singles champion received $564,000. In 1997, when the prize money reached a record $11.2, the Wimbledon men's champion received $676,450, while the women's champ got $608,805. Defending this discriminatory policy, All England Club chairman John Curry said: "We. . . feel we have no good reason to change from where we are. . . . It is still the public's view that they prefer the men's matches to the women's." We wonder where he's getting *his* information. But as far as the pay inequities: "That mean(s)," explains Martina Navratilova, "a relatively obscure player, Richard Krajicek, who up to then could only have sold tickets in the Netherlands, (i)s paid more than a superstar, Steffi Graf, who could sell tickets in Timbuktu."[2]

Navratilova says that some rationalize the pay inequity by saying that women only play a best-of-three-set format, while the men play a best-of-five. "All right," she says. "If that is the reason, let's change it." Women, she says, should play the best-of-five-set format. Such a change could help the women's tour, by taking nerves and luck out of the equation. The longer the match, she says, the better the chance top players have to win. "Women aren't delicate creatures," she says. "We won't get tired." Graf, Seles, Gabriella Sabatini, and Anke Huber have all played five-set matches. "They produced their best tennis in the fifth set and lived to tell about it."

And Navratilova should know about the inequities, and overcoming them. She defected to the U.S. from Czechoslovakia at a time when the top male player earned 50 percent more than the top female. But just as Babe Didrikson-Zaharias changed perceptions about female golfers, Navratilova changed perceptions about female tennis players and female athletes in general. She lifted weights and cross-trained. She won 167 singles events, including nine Wimbledon and four U.S. Open titles. She was the first female athlete to earn more than a million dollars in one year; in 1984, she won 74 consecutive matches and $2,173,556 in prize money — higher competitive earnings than any athlete in the world, except for three boxers. Throughout her career, she has earned more than $20 million dollars from tennis tournaments alone.[3]

While Navratilova has made the world a better place for female athletes, while work done by the Women's Sports Foundation and other advocates has improved the status of female athletes and made female endorsements somewhat more common, that arena remains predominantly male and endorsement dollars by the multi-millions are given primarily to male athletes. The ever-popular Jackie Joyner-Kersee — often described as the greatest female athlete alive — has been comparatively successful in endorsements, but she is a rarity. Bonnie Blair — the winningest American (male or female) in Winter Olympic history and the first American female to win five Olympic gold medals (either Winter or Summer Games) — had to be a savvy businesswoman in order to promote herself just to raise enough money for travel and training expenses. Finally, after winning her fifth gold medal, she can book speaking engagements for $15,000.

When Lyn St. James realized that she had talent as a driver that would allow her to become a professional, she quickly found that she had little leverage. In an exceptionally expensive sport, she had to convince both officials and supporters of auto racing that she should not only be allowed to compete but that she deserved to be bankrolled. What saved her, she told us, was perseverance. "I figured out in 1979, my first year as a pro, that I was going to have to sell. I owned an auto parts business, and I had to sell a lot of shock absorbers. And I had to sell myself as a potential moneymaker to companies which were really only interested in the bottom line." Based on her research, St. James concluded that she and the Ford Motor Company were made for each other: Ford was trying to sell more of their products to women, and St. James, an incredibly accomplished woman driver, needed a serious sponsor. She began a two-year telephone and letter-writing campaign to persuade Ford to sponsor her. When Ford finally signed her in 1981, she traveled 250 days a year as a spokesperson in order to keep her sponsor.

Thanks to women like St. James, Navratilova, Blair, and Joyner-Kersee, a new day is dawning for female athletes. Sheryl Swoopes, for example, is the first woman to have her own shoe line — NIKE's Air Swoopes. Publicity about, and interest in, today's female athletes (Gail Devers and Gwen Torrence, for example) seems to be increasing dramatically.

Nike runs a 30-second commercial in which adolescent girls of all shapes, sizes, and ethnic backgrounds say (in clips):

> "If you let me play. . . if you let me play sports, I will like myself more, I will have more confidence, if you let me play sports.
>
> "If you let me play sports, if you let me play, I will be 60 percent less likely to get breast cancer. I will suffer less depression.
>
> "If you let me play sports, I will be more likely to leave a man who beats me, if you let me play. . . .
>
> "If you let me play sports, I will be less likely to get pregnant before I want to. I'll learn what it means to be strong. . . to be strong. . . if you let me play."

Twenty-five years after Title IX was signed into law, we are beginning to see the results of what happens when we let girls and women play. We are moving closer to a generation of girls who cannot imagine *NOT* having full competitive opportunities — although 90 percent of schools and colleges are not in compliance with Title IX and the NCAA says it will take another decade to reach full compliance.

Companies like Lady Foot Locker, Reebok, Oceanspray, Avon, and Tampax have donated large amounts of money for women's athletics, and to send the message to "excel on and off the playing field." And as Lopiano wrote in an article for *Women's Sports & Fitness*, "Other media entities are beginning to embrace female athletes as champions, heroes and role models. Major corporations like State Farm Insurance, General Motors, Visa and Kodak are using female athletes in large-scale advertising and promotional campaigns. The wonderful byproduct of all this is that the corporate commitment to female consumers is fueling gender equity in women's sports salaries."[4]

With the help of inspirational women such as those mentioned throughout this book and organizations such as the Women's Sports Foundation and the Winter Sports Foundation, the barriers that impede girls and women are steadily being knocked down. With more and more women like The Fabulous Sports Babe, Pam Oliver, Joan Ryan, Christine Brennen, and Lydia Stephans (vice president of ABC Sports) moving into the forefront of the media, accurate and equal information will be given to a growing, demanding audience. Soon, we hope, remarks like those made by CBS announcer Ben Wright about female golfers' breast sizes and sexual preferences will not be tolerated (as his were).

It was those very remarks that made The Fabulous Sports Babe wonder out loud, "Why was he on the golf tour? And why are men still coaching women's NCAA?" There are so many qualified women to coach at the collegiate level. Why are the coaching positions still dominated by men?

Why, when there are women like Pat Summit, head coach of the national champion women's basketball team at University of Tennessee? Under Summit's coaching, the Lady Volunteers have won back-to-back national championships, and have won five since 1987. Summit is second on the all-time list of coaches with the most national titles, trailing only John Wooden of UCLA. She also coached American teams to gold in the 1979 World Championships and the 1984 Olympics. Hard to argue with those numbers.

But Anita DeFrantz, U.S. representative to the International Olympic Committee, explains how a key U.S. gender equity law actually helped men into coaching women's teams. "Title IX became enforced and colleges realized they had to come up with the money [for women's sports], but men were in charge," she says. "It was and still is in many cases an old boy network. Once the money came in for coaching positions for women's teams, men wanted the women's coaching jobs. At the time, women had no experience."

In Columbus, Ohio, WNCI-FM reporter Romona Holloway hosts the show "BackTalk" early Sunday mornings. In July 1996, she had as a guest Brian Agler, new head coach of the Columbus Quest women's basketball team. Holloway commented that women should be coached by women — suggesting that while there are plenty of great male coaches, there are also plenty of great female coaches, and that women understand women a little better. A point that can't really be argued, yet a caller named Skip did so. He complained that women want everything now, that just because someone is a woman didn't necessarily make her the better coach for the job. "Women's sports aren't just for women," he pointed out. "Look at me, I'm a huge Buckeye fan."

"Oh, so you've been to the Lady Buckeye games?" Holloway asked.

"Uh, no, I've never been to a ladies' game."

"Okay, would you go to an ABL game?" Holloway persisted. Silence.

"No, I probably wouldn't."

While DeFrantz feels confident that coaching positions are becoming increasingly available to women, the Fabulous Sports Babe isn't satisfied. Progress is moving too slowly for her. But, then, the Babe isn't one to sit around and wait for things to happen. Having been in the sports business for more than 15 years, she is the first woman to have an all-sports radio show with ESPN, and the first to have a national show — a show she is proud to say has a totally different format than her competition. Rather than have "bull sessions" with caller/listeners, the Babe's show has a heavy screening process before someone gets on the show. Before anyone goes on her airwaves, the Babe knows the person's name, where he or she is calling from, and what the caller's comment will be. That's all anyone can make — a comment. Then, the Babe hangs up and moves on to the next caller. This format keeps the program fast-paced and hugely successful.

The Babe is up at the crack of dawn, pouring over seven different sports papers, looking over anything that's come in on the wire, and checking out the sports channels before she goes on the air. The Babe studies all this sports material, she says, "because I am a woman; I have to be ten times better. I've invaded *their* domain." The Babe is continuously called by "fans" who test her, quiz her knowledge of sports — any sport. And she is always up for the challenge. "It's not fair, but I have to work harder, and it never leaves me that I cannot let anyone down. I'm the only woman doing this [at this level]. If I can't, they'll say 'See, a woman can't do it'."

As good as she is, there are still some who cannot accept the idea of a woman hosting a sports show. Despite being called every name in the book, the Babe has a sense of humor about it all. "They call me. They call me, and I keep thinking, if you don't like the channel, change it. But they can't. They keep listening." At a Seattle SuperSonics basketball game, an angry fan sought the Babe out, jerked her arm to the side, and said, "You bitch! You hung up on me four times!" She politely removed her arm from his hand and asked, "Why the f--- did you call back the next three?"

While she talks the talk of games, her job is no game. The Babe has fine-tuned the timing, the nuances of talking sports, going into breaks, cutting off those callers who want to interrupt her carefully orchestrated symphony. Atlanta Falcons public relations assistant director Frank Kleha says he is a regular listener of The Fabulous Sports Babe's show. It is the very format she is proud of which draws Kleha. "It's fast-paced; you don't get bogged down with all the chat. It's a show I'd like to get my players on."

Tom Rothmann, a sports marketing director in Columbus, is in awe of the Babe. He has a picture of the Babe sitting on his desk and teases, "If I was ever on her show I would say, "Mother, I am home!" For Rothmann, the Babe *is* the best. The four-hour talk show — the first nationally syndicated sports program with a woman as a host — is aired over 190 radio stations and ESPN2, the cable network. Nanci "The Babe" Donnellan alone breaks into the traditional male domain of sports every day.

To everyone's benefit, barriers also are being knocked down in the non-sports workplace. Knocked down as women assume more executive leadership roles: women like Secretary of State Madeline Albright, Carol Bellamy at UNICEF, Catherine Bertini of the World Food Program, and Sadoka Ogata at the U.N. High Commission for Refugees. Just in the United Nations system, five of the major agencies are led by women, demonstrating not only that they, as individuals, are qualified and capable, but that women in general are capable. These women are not exceptions to the rule. They *are* the rule, the rule for the coming millenium — that women and men are equal, and that women are strong, capable, and ready. And as more women convince men of this simple truth, more women will begin to believe and embrace it, and it will become reality.

Until then, though, perhaps we need to adopt the ways of Didrikson-Zaharias. It certainly works for males. If one watches adolescent and teenage boys on a basketball court or in the gym, it's hard not to notice the bragging, big-talking bravado that goes on. Mostly amusing, this banter goes back and forth, while two or more wager on someone's abilities, while they good-heartedly challenge one another to some athletic feat. This is largely unknown in the female community. Bravado is a rarity. But wouldn't we have more attention from both media and corporate sponsors if we took a kind of Didrikson-Zaharias approach? Wouldn't it be hard not to be noticed on the court or in the gym if we loudly proclaimed great athletic prowess, if we predicted great athletic feats?

We tested this theory, and in the words of our friend Tia Trent, one of the co-authors got "lip-witted" with a trainer from Accelerate Ohio. Working on a difficult treadmill routine, Alex was nearing the end of her training session and preparing to take a speed test. Alex loudly proclaimed to the trainer that she *would* run 18 miles per hour on the treadmill.

Two things happened: 1) Alex ran the 18 miles per hour, proving once again that self-esteem and confidence are the ticket to success, and 2) the entire gym cheered her on. Some of the boys we had labeled as cocky encouraged Alex. All the trainers yelled, telling her to keep up her speed and, when she was done, everyone was smiling, and there were many "congratulations" and high-fives. In and of itself, this was a small feat (especially since many of the guys present could run 20 miles per hour), but it was huge in the sense that boys and girls, men and women stopped their own work-outs or training to watch and cheer one woman onward toward her publicly-proclaimed goal!

Linda Robertson, president of the Association for Women in Sports Media, writes: "Someday when women are coaching in the NBA, playing in their own pro leagues, color commentating on Monday Night Football, presiding over the International Olympic Committee, earning college scholarships in proportion to their numbers, and running the world's biggest shoe company, we'll look back on the 20th century as ancient history."[5]

Until then, though, only as the female community pulls together, will equity slowly replace exclusion, and the need to stand in Times Square peddling bumper stickers fade.

"Hi, Babe? This is Rick. I'm a first-time caller," says a voice over the airwaves.

The Babe coos, "Come to Mother."

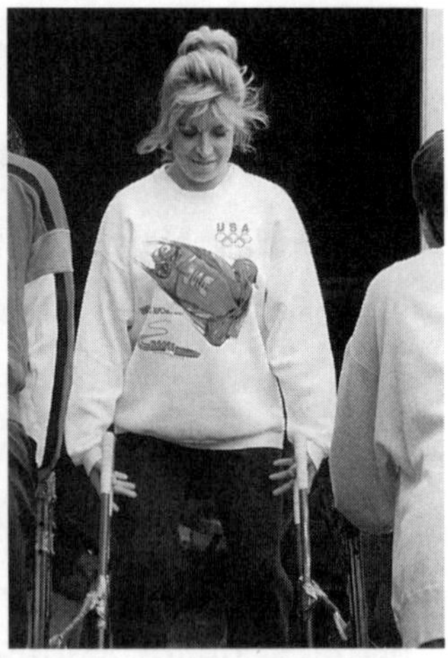

What funding from bumper stickers can accomplish: Alex and Liz prepare a sled in Calgary (upper left); Alex with coach Steve Maiorca at Push Camp (left); Michelle and Laurie Millet represent the U.S. Women Bobsledders for the first time internationally in St. Moritz, Switzerland (below); Michelle at Push Camp — Lake Placid (above).

Chapter Eight

Toting the Chain

You got to fight them. . .
I can't do it for you.
You got to fight them for yourself.

— Alice Walker, *The Color Purple*

When U.S. speedskater Pooch Harrington participated in the 1960 Olympic Games at Squaw Valley, the temperature outside was -25° F. A blizzard was brewing, dumping snow faster than the snow crews could clear the ice rinks (there were no indoor rinks then).

Because skating was impossible, the U.S. speedskating coach sent the male skaters inside to clean their skates, stretch, and keep warm. He sent the female skaters on a hiking excursion to the top of the ski jump. This coach had made it clear that he didn't want women on his team. He had "no idea what to do with us," says Harrington. So he routinely sent them on wild-goose chases just to keep them busy and out of his hair.

Angered by this newest and ludicrous chore, a member of the women's team — to protest the coach's ruling as unfair — picked up a heavy chain that decorated a restaurant in the Olympic village. Amused with the symbolism of the chain and their first act of passive defiance, the members of the first women's speedskating team began trudging up the mountain carrying the heavy chain over their shoulders, feeling a tiny bit vindicated. Some two hours later, as the storm worsened, the temperature dropped, and the wind and snow whipped them, the humor had worn off. The chain had become incredibly cold and heavy, but they couldn't put it down because it didn't belong to them.

Cursing their teammate's bright idea and every blistering step, they plunged on literally chained together until they were at last rescued by a park ranger. Although they may have been too tired and cold to realize it, the chain, as it became increasingly burdensome, had also become increasingly symbolic of their status and the sexism that confined them.

Despite the weather turning on them, the women's team had the right idea by handling their adversity and discrimination with humor. At the time, they had no legal recourse, so attitude and determination were all-important. Women's sports history is filled with stories, like this one, of those who — through grit, determination, and positive attitudes — have won (and are winning) victories, not only for themselves, not only for other female athletes, but for all women.

We feel this way about our own bobsled athletes. The opening of Park City, Utah, was to be a joyous occasion. The site of the 2002 Olympic Games, Park City boasts only the second bobsled track in the United States and the only one on which, by most regards, any sane person would want to slide. Female bobsledders went to the opening ceremonies — having been *promised* the opportunity to slide and take part in the opening ceremonies.

What we had hoped for and what actually happened were two entirely different things. The brochure handed out to spectators did not even mention the U.S. women's bobsled team. What it did do, however, was name the youth program — an *unofficial* program to which the the U.S. women's team had donated $5,000. This was $5,000 we really needed, but we felt so strongly about trying to involve youths, particularly young girls, in the federation that we bit the bullet. As a result of that donation, two members of our competitive team were <u>not</u> able to compete in Germany.

Worse, we have been told that Utah Sports Authority — the folks (some of whom are women) who run the Park City track — refuses to acknowledge women bobsledders. A sled which we had *paid* to have repaired and in running shape for the opening ceremonies lay untouched and abandoned, far from the repair shed. Sliding times were changed and then cancelled. The women athletes there had taken the semester off from school, or leaves of absence from their jobs to stand around for two weeks. But always they showed up at the track with bright smiles, determined not to let the politics get to them.

"Every day I watched their hearts break, but every day they came with fresh hopes," said a spectator who attended the opening ceremonies. The women helped the men move sleds, retrieved equipment, and shoveled snow from the sled area so the men could work on their sleds.

This was certainly not the first time that women bobsledders had been so deceived. During the '94-95 season, women on the national team were repeatedly promised ice time in Lake Placid (by the federation head coach and the federation executive director) only to pay for airline tickets, fly there, and be told that there was no ice time. This happened not once, but three times. During the '95-96 season, the women were told that we must come to Lake Placid for a national qualifying race, although we would probably have no housing and no sleds. During the '96-97 season, we were promised a coach for an international race in Calgary, only to be told before the race by that coach that he had no time for us and that we were on our own (not the first time we had heard that). We have a "team" director who withholds critical sponsorship money, information about competitions, and exposure to the press from team members not in his favor, regardless of their standing on the team.

The discrimination continues, but we do not give up. If anything, such discrimination makes us more dedicated, more determined to persevere. We are simply demonstrating the lessons taught by so many great female athletes who survived great adversity.

In an interview with ESPN before her death in 1994, the great Wilma Rudolph told how she was recruited from her small town in Clarksville, Tennessee, to attend Tennessee State, some 45 minutes away. Only 13 years old, Wilma had never been away from home. It was her first bus ride, her first adventure. "It was only 45 minutes away, but you would have thought I was going to Europe." Sports had opened a whole new world — a world beyond the racism and poverty of her youth. Just the burning desire to run was enough to raise Rudolph, who had suffered from polio, from her bed and propel her on to become a champion.

In 1960, after the Olympic Games in Rome, Rudolph returned to Clarksville an American hero and three-time gold medalist. The entire town celebrated her homecoming, but before she would agree to a banquet in her honor, she insisted that there be no segregation. It was the first time blacks and whites sat together in Clarksville, and it would be a night the town would never forget. Sport allowed this young woman — at least for one night — to control her world and set it right.

For Althea Gibson, times were very hard at home so she did almost anything she could to stay outside — away from her own home life. In sporting history, she broke the color barrier for tennis and golf, the more prestigious "white" sports. But in terms of one little girl who was trying to avoid a horrible home life and find herself, sport was her answer. "I was determined to be somebody, even if it killed me," she said.

As all athletes know, sports aren't all fun. It's always hard work, often physically painful, and sometimes, as we see with the 1960 women's speedskating team, emotionally demanding and even demeaning. While humor is often a good way to deal with adversity, there are times when the problems reach a point that require further action, when humor isn't sufficient or appropriate in dealing with the situation, despite the most positive attitude.

Years after the experiences of Rudolph and Gibson and the 1960 speedskaters, Julie Croteau chose a legal battle when she had exhausted all other options. By then, the 1972 education bill, Title IX, had been signed into legislation, mandating full equality for women's school athletics (although it hasn't ensured equity). Croteau's lawsuit was the right course of action for her, enabling her to become a pioneer for women in baseball and to achieve some of her own aspirations. She has said that at the time she and her friends knew that they were right to be willing to fight for equity, and she is still sure today. Croteau concedes she "failed and succeeded publicly." While she lost her case in court, she won in life. "Fight the good battle — even if you can lose." Croteau is a visionary. She sees women in all sports with nothing but ourselves to hold us back. Now with the MLB, she worked as a broadcaster during the 1997 All-Star game and during the World Series.

And then there's 11-year-old Keesha Williams of Grove City, Ohio. When told she couldn't play basketball with the neighborhood boys because she was a girl, Keesha marched up to the oldest boy, punched him in the nose, and poked a finger in his chest, telling him she *would* play and she *would* beat the pants off him. "I did, too!" she told us proudly. Of course, we don't condone violence in any way, *but we wish we had seen that*. Knowing when to fight, and who, and how, and knowing when to go-along-to-get-along were primary concerns of the athletes we interviewed. The majority said they believe that fighting for rights is important, but "choosing the right battle" is more important. Contrary to the advice of the ex-ESPN executive, the athletes were not concerned about choosing a battle because it could be won, but rather choosing a battle — when all other options had been exhausted — because principle is at stake.

Attorney Ed Williams, former Olympian, co-founder of the Athletes' Committee to the USOC, and an athlete-rights advocate, agrees that principles must be protected, even if the road to equality is a rocky one. "You can't make any forward progress," he says, "if you are not willing to fight difficult battles. One recognizes the political reality that some cannot be won right now, but that does not mean they should not be fought. Some athletes choose to be leaders in these difficult situations. The battle may not be won for several years." But, he points out, legal battles set precedents and very often raise the awareness necessary to overturn earlier, discriminatory decisions. So the battles must be fought.

As in marketing, not knowing what to do about discrimination can keep women from acting. Inequality and inequity in sports exist at all levels — from elementary school to the national level. So, Williams stresses, girls must learn and understand the law before they can decide if they are willing or able to take on court challenges. For instance, female athletes should be acquainted with the American Sports Act of 1979, U.S. Code 36, Section 391. Williams refers to this important legislation as "the foundation of the U.S. Olympic Committee charter." Another important document is the USOC Constitution, particularly Article IX, which deals with the right of the athlete to compete.

Emphasizing Williams' advice to know the law, Woodhull (of the Media Studies Center) was quick to point out, "In years to come, historians of the women's movement may well define Title IX as the most important legislation in re-defining women's ability to succeed in a broad variety of endeavors."

Beyond knowing the rights that females have guaranteed to them under the law, Williams stresses that girls and women must have the courage to take a stand for what they believe, the courage to be unpopular. Having a thick skin can be difficult, and Williams says that while the law is often on the side of the women, most are too afraid to act, fearing repercussions. After all, Croteau became an outcast in her high school after her lawsuit. We know this all too well in the sport of bobsledding. Not all athletes are trailblazers. Not every athlete is going to be willing to speak out for the good of the team, which is frustrating for those who are.

Speaking out as an athlete is difficult, fearing repercussions from coaches, federations, sponsors, fellow athletes. We accept that not everyone is going to be a Billie Jean King, a Fabulous Sports Babe, or a Liz Parr-Smestad. But we would hope in the spirit of team, of sisterhood, of pride, that while one might not be able to speak out, she would always support those who do.

Particularly in women's sports which are fighting for equal status, such as Olympic status, women need to pull together as a whole.

There are still nine Olympic sports which remain one-sex-only: bobsledding, Nordic ski jumping, pentathlon, boxing, weightlifting, wrestling, and water polo are all men-only, and synchronized swimming and rhythmic gymnastics are women-only. Speaking for bobsledding, Olympic exclusion is particularly hard to understand, and learning that we will still be excluded from the 2002 Games was bitter medicine to swallow.

A federation, the U.S. Bobsled and Skeleton Federation, already exists. There are already training facilities, coaches, equipment, and staff. Women are not asking for a new federation, or new facilities; we only want to have equal representation in an already-existing, already-funded sport. But our federation is not so willing to share the wealth between the sexes. And while the USOC says there is no money for additional athletes, totally new sports such as snowboarding *are* added to the Olympic Games.

That pill is hard to swallow, and the logic difficult to understand. And with only one woman on the executive board of the International Olympic Committee (IOC) — the committee that decides the inclusion *or exclusion* of a sport — women's voices are weak.

We asked that one woman, Anita DeFrantz, what has to be done to get men-only sports expanded to include women in the Games (and women-only sports expanded to men).

"A certain number of championships must be held for the IOC to review [the sport]," De Frantz says. "It is up to the women to champion their sports. Only the federations representing each sport can make requests to the IOC, so it is important that the women move the federations." But moving the federations is not easy.

DeFrantz does not take the role of "the only woman" lightly. She has labored to elevate women into the decision-making levels of the sporting world. In 1995, DeFrantz spearheaded the IOC policy mandating that women must make up at least 10 percent of the board by the year 2000, as well as 10 percent of the boards of all 197 National Olympic Committees. By the year 2005, DeFrantz intends to see that number rise to 20 percent. As Lopiano of the Women's Sports Foundation says, these numbers, although they seem small, will have profound and positive consequences.

DeFrantz is also responsible for a 1989 study of television coverage of men's and women's sports events in the U.S. That study, entitled "Gender Stereotyping and Televised Sports," proved to be very valuable, indeed, showing the overwhelming male bias in sports coverage. In 1994, a newer, updated study was conducted, outlining the same problems. "Those two studies have significantly changed women's sports for the better," Lopiano says.

Currently, DeFrantz runs the Amateur Athletic Foundation (which manages Southern California's endowment from the 1984 Olympic Games), and serves on the IOC board, the Salt Lake City Olympic Organizing Committee, and nearly a dozen other foundation boards. But she took the time from her incredibly busy schedule to speak with us. Her advice, succinctly stated, is: "Know when to fight and when to walk away." No one believes more firmly in the need for powerful female leadership than DeFrantz, and no one knows better when to fight.

"What do you mean we? Where were "we" when I was out there busting my rear?" -- Anita DeFrantz (shown here training with her teammates) challenges the U.S. government's decision to boycott the 1980 Moscow Games.

In 1980, when the United States boycotted the Moscow Games, DeFrantz, then a rowing athlete, fought back. DeFrantz first heard about the boycott when a reporter from *Sports Illustrated* called her for her reaction. "They (*Sports Illustrated)* said, 'We're boycotting the Games' and I said, 'Who's we? What do you mean we? Where were *we* when I was out there busting my rear?'" The White House claimed to be held hostage by world events — by the Soviet invasion of Afghanistan; Carter administration officials said there was no other choice. "But I wondered," DeFrantz says, "whose lives would they really change? I'll tell you who, only the 500 U.S. athletes who didn't get to participate. It did nothing to change the Soviet [occupation] in Afghanistan. . . . Meanwhile, a scientific convention was held in Moscow with representatives from the United States, and we continued selling wheat to the Soviets. It was all very wrong."

While the boycott and the Moscow Games proceeded without DeFrantz and her fellow American athletes, DeFrantz earned the Olympic Order Medal of Bronze for her leadership role in fighting the boycott. It was a fight that pushed her to the forefront, giving her a reputation that the International Olympic Committee took very seriously. DeFrantz recognizes she is where she is today because of the stand she took.

For bobsledding, the barriers are still in front of us. Before women's bobsledding can be admitted to the Olympic agenda, the IOC and FIBT need to feel comfortable with the abilities and safety of the women sliders. Certainly, the admission of women's hockey into the 1998 Nagano Games has shown us the IOC's eagerness for gender equity. Women's hockey was admitted to the Olympic Games with only eight participating countries. For bobsledding, the number of participating countries is not so much a problem as getting ice time for the women to become competent drivers and brakes.

In 1996, while FIBT officials heavily scrutinized races held in Winterberg, Germany, and St. Moritz, Switzerland, there were more serious crashes than there had been on the international circuit in years. In St. Moritz alone, two sleds (one Swiss, one German) flew out of the track and the Swiss teammates had to be rescued by helicopter from the trees. The result: the Swiss closed their track to the women, claiming women are unsafe sledders. (Nevermind that male sliders have died on that track —one decapitated. The track was never closed to men.) When tracks become unavailable to the women, there will be even less practice and more crashes. It is a double-edged sword.

DeFrantz's encouragement to women to "move the federations" also is a double-edged sword. Without Olympic status, these sports will continue to get little to no support from their federations, and without financial support from the federations there can be no real international championships — meaning no Olympic status. As with the women who trudged in chains up a Squaw Valley mountain, the burden on women in currently non-Olympic status national sports has become increasingly heavy. Many of these athletes, understandably, give up.

Case-in-point: in 1994, when the Modern Pentathlon Federation was informed that women would not be included in the 1996 Summer Olympics, the federation cut funds to the women. "We feel it was wrong [for women not to be included in the Games]," says Dean Billick, the federation's executive director. "There is no legitimate reason for it." But once the ruling was handed down, he says, the federation had to protect its resources for those athletes invited to the 1996 Games — the men.

What happened after that is no surprise. Female pentathletes were forced to stop training full-time so that they could return to work full-time. Many have lost hope. "They lost their goals and stopped [training]," Billick says. The federation continues to pay for the women's travel and coaching expenses to international competitions, but the painful reality is that in a sport as demanding as modern pentathlon, it is virtually impossible to be serious contenders with only part-time training.

Female bobsledders understand that dilemma all too well. And we constantly hear the unfounded complaint that any money spent on us (despite the fact that we have a corporate sponsor) is taking money from the men's program. It is a familiar complaint.

In fact, one of the arguments frequently used *against* gender equity in sports (particularly at the college level) is that, in providing more opportunities for female athletes, we reduce monetary support for the sports that are the most popular (i.e., men's sports) and bring in the most money. That money, opponents of gender equity point out, is what supports all sports. The argument goes that if the football program loses money, then there will be less for everyone.

In fairness, we rarely heard this argument from athletes themselves. It is usually the coaches, particularly at high school and college levels, who are still convinced that funding equal athletic opportunities for women will decimate their men's programs.

Lopiano notes that while women's programs are being accused of taking money for football scholarships and/or weakening all the other athletic programs, it is the "women who have less than 36 percent of all athletic participation opportunities, 33 percent of all scholarship dollars, 24 percent of sport budgets, and 23 percent of recruiting budgets."

Other little-known facts about "golden goose" athletic programs, i.e., football and basketball:

- At about 80 percent of all NCAA (National Collegiate Athletic Association) member institutions, football does not pay for women's sports or even for itself.
- Among the supposedly lucrative big-time football programs in Division I-A, 33 percent are running deficit programs averaging losses of more than $1,000,000 annually.
- Ninety-five percent of Division I-AA football programs are running deficits averaging about $600,000 per year.
- Thirty-two percent of all Division I-A men's basketball programs run deficits averaging more than $200,000 a year.
- Eighty-one percent of all other Division I men's basketball programs run annual deficits of close to $270,000.[1]

As Lopiano says, "There are no golden geese. There are only fat geese eating the food that could fund additional athletic opportunities for women." And as Women's Sports Foundation president Benita Fitzgerald Mosley says: "If college presidents and athletic directors cut superfluous costs in men's football and basketball, enough funding could be available for everyone. Those well-funded sports simply have to give up small portions of their budgets so that both women and men involved in non-revenue sports can have a chance to play. The point of an anti-discrimination law is to bring the disadvantaged population up to the level of the advantaged population, not to bring an already advantaged population down."[2]

Donna Lopiano

Which brings us back to knowing when, who, and how to fight. Female athletes must educate themselves about the law — not only state and federal laws, but also bylaws specific to individual federations. They must have the facts at hand to negate the old, invalid arguments made by those who fear for themselves and oppose expanding athletic opportunities. Female athletes must be aware that discrimination (and the inevitably resulting harassment) exists at all levels, and they must be prepared for dealing with that discrimination.

We all must continue to encourage girls and women not to give up; we should take pride in those spirits who do not. As American Gladiator Sky says, "When I die, I don't want to die saying 'I wish I would have. . . .'"

We can all take a few lessons from Olympic fencer Cheris who refuses to acknowledge the word "can't." At our Accelerate Ohio program, the word "can't" hangs on a poster in front of the treadmill. There is a line through the word as though it were obscene. But when you are running 16-plus miles per hour at a 30-degree incline, the word "can't" seems dangerously real. There are times when "can't" is the only word that comes to mind. Yet, Cheris refuses to accept this.

During the 1992 Barcelona Games, while Olympians traveled to Barcelona to prove themselves, Cheris and her colleagues were sent to Cuba. Epee (Cheris' form of fencing) was not yet an Olympic sport. That is when Cheris began her campaign. She was told over and over that it would not become an Olympic sport. "I didn't hear that," she says. "You just don't. If you believe in your sport, in yourself, you make the sport media-worthy, give demonstrations, write letters, call all the fencing clubs you can.... It got to the point people were calling me saying, 'Elaine, please, stop the letters!'

"The easiest thing," she says, "is to say it can't be done. You must decide where you are going and *do it*." But when we marveled at her very positive attitude, Cheris was quick to point out that it's not all about focusing on the positive. Learning to channel the negative can lead to success. "It's not about crashing through walls all the time. First, look for the door, asking yourself, 'Where am I going; where am I going?' When you've looked and find there are no doors, then you can work on making one." Negativity, she says, can work to your advantage, making you work harder and want it more. Wanting it and working for it may be the keys to success, but some doors have old and very stubborn locks. Cheris' point: make new doors.

When the bobsled federation recently held a "pee-wee" bobsled competition for children under 16 years of age, two preadolescent sisters entered. They raced against twelve all-boy teams. At the end of the meet, the excited girls and their parents listened to the times of the boys' teams and tallied up the scores. The girls had come in fourth place! Then, right before their eyes, the judges changed the scores, placing the girls in tenth place. Welcome to bobsledding, girls.

Originally, bobsledding was a mixed sport that required women team members. Yet as early as 1924, women began to be banned from competition. In 1940, the Amateur Athletic Union (AAU) reopened the sport to women. Katharin Dewey (granddaughter of Melvile Dewey, creator of the Dewey Decimal library catalog system) won the U.S. National Four-Man Bobsled Championship. In doing so, Dewey became the *only* woman in the history of bobsledding, or any other amateur sport, to win a national championship in open competition against men. Days later, the AAU reversed its decision and ruled that women could compete only against other women, stripping Dewey of her title and effectively banning her from the sport.

Just as the spirit to compete thrives in the current U.S. women's bobsled team, so it does in a new generation of bobsledders. Rather than quit, one of the sisters in the pee-wee competition turned to her father and said, "I guess I'll just have to come in first place next time." When asked why she continues to bobsled, she says, wide-eyed, as if there could be no other explanation, "Because I love it."

These are two girls we hope will ride the wave of adolescent peer pressure and continue to focus their determination into quiet storms of progress. What so many do not understand — like the grown men who stripped two children of fourth place because of sexism — is that this is not a boys-against-the-girls story. We are all in this together, athletes striving to do our personal bests and to enhance our sports and ourselves.

Still, when it is boys against the girls, girls fare pretty well. For example, during a sparring workout, Denise Perdue watched as her husband, David, took a pretty hard hit from a rambunctious sparring partner. In Tae Kwon Do, maintaining physical control and restraint is part of the training. But some athletes (often male) believe lack of control is confirmation of their abilities and power. When it was Denise's turn to spar with the same student, she told us, "I had only been sparring a few months and the [guy] thought that sparring me, a woman, a green belt, would be a breeze. At the beginning of the match, he did some weird move, from another martial art, like that starting stance in *The Karate Kid*. He was mocking me. I proceeded to knock his glasses from his face onto the floor." Needless to say, he did not underestimate Perdue again. When she returned to her husband's side, she remarked, "I got him back for you, honey."

In her article "The Girls Against the Boys," adventurer-turned-journalist Sarah Odell describes the frustrations she felt being excluded from the Team American Pride troop: a team that consisted of five members, one of whom had to be a female.[3]

Despite its title, the article is not about girls against boys, but women striking out on their own. For Odell, when she was cut at try-outs, she and four other women created their own team — the first ever all-female team.

For what? The sixth annual Raid Gauloises (Challenge of the Warriors), said to be the most extreme race in the world. It is an event that demands that the teams hike, bike, climb, raft, and drag themselves to the finish line after managing 223 miles of incredibly crude terrain — in this case, in Bornea.

But before they could endure the extreme fatigue, leeches, reptiles, insects, torrential downpours, and sleepless nights, the first challenge for the women was to find a sponsor for the needed $40,000 to fund the excursion. Team American Pride Woman found support from Swiss Army Brands, and they were on their way.

Often lost in the Bornean wilds, the women knew many were counting them out. Odell confesses to giving in to defeatist thinking — that is, until they discovered that Team American Pride (the U.S. men's team) had been disqualified. No longer were the women competing against their male rivals. Now it meant finishing for their sponsor, for America, for themselves.

The odds seemed insurmountable. One teammate fell with dysentery — Bornea's revenge. Hooked to an IV drip to hydrate her, the teammate rallied the following day, allowing the entire team to move on. Clawing their way through caves, biking up mountains, canoeing through the rapids, 7 days and 22 hours later, the first all-female team and only the second American team ever to complete the Raid Gauloises crossed the finish lines. They didn't win, but it never was about that.

Anna Seaton-Huntington, two-time Olympic rower and member of the America^3 team, asked and answered the rhetorical question, "What did women prove?" by competing in the America's Cup race.

"The 'real winners' are the people who cross the finish line first," Seaton-Huntington says. "That was not us. We did not sail flawlessly.... But the women's team did exhibit an enormous amount of courage when we went out on the course totally green to face off against men who had been sailing in America's Cups all their adult lives....

"Most likely there will never be another [all-female] team in the America's Cup. But we hope that as a result of our efforts, there will be women on what would once have been all-male crews. As my teammates and I go on with our lives, as sailors, rocket scientists, mothers, hotel managers or journalists, we will know that we have made inroads into a spectacular, once spectacularly male, sport."[4]

Our wanting to participate in sports does not mean we want to beat the boys, or join the "boys' club." We just want to be allowed to play also. We want to push ourselves to be better, to feel the satisfaction of accomplishment, to feel the sky is the limit, to learn the competitive skills needed in business. We want to demonstrate as Sameka Randall, the Associated Press' Ms. Basketball, says: "We can hang."

Chapter Nine

Entering the Boys' Club

When we refer to "the boys' club," we have in mind those areas of society where male domination has had the effect of excluding women, whether intentionally or not. Obviously, sport is one of those areas. The military is another.

"Don't tell me that the Pentagon or White House or some other idiot said we can't deploy women soldiers to Grenada because if they don't go, then my unit can't go. We are a team. They are essential to my ability to accomplish the mission."

— Anonymous battalion commander, XVIII Airborne Corps, 1983

Our father, Marc Powe, a retired career Army officer, sees a connection between women in sports crossing gender lines and the barriers he saw women cross during his service from 1961 to 1991. "When I entered the Army, there were not many women to be found," Powe says. "The [female] officers were invariably either nurses or administrators, while female NCOs always had clerical or medical duties. By the early 1970s, though, women had leapt over those fences. They had gained acceptance in a wide range of duties, including signal, military intelligence, and military police specialties, which did several things at once. Now, for the first time, they were in the mainstream of the Army. Equally important, they were able to have careers which are normal in the military services: they could alternate between specialist and generalist duties, receive the same military education and training as their male peers, and begin to aspire for the coveted senior ranks of colonel and general, although that was still a decade away."

None of this was easy, and many male soldiers, whether officers, NCOs or junior enlisteds, disapproved strongly. Dozens of reasons were offered by the Army's leadership (and that of the other services, which were also experiencing rapid changes in the roles of their female members) for why women could only go to this gate, to that level, or to other artificial limits. Significantly, little of the serious concern being expressed was about physical capability such as upper body strength or monthly cycles. Instead, the credible questioning was about societal values and appropriateness.

Congressional and public opinion recoiled at the idea of women in combat. The mere possibility that women might be in foxholes caused anxiety from Capitol Hill to the Pentagon to the Army in the field. "I believe that most male soldiers were genuinely afraid of what might happen to women if exposed to enemy infantry," says Powe. "Sexist or not, few men wanted to think about their daughters, wives, or any other women subjected to the increasingly lethal weapons of the modern battlefield, let alone the possibility of capture, rape, and the like. There was plenty of defensive male chauvinism as well — the idea that 'if some woman can do what I'm doing, then that means I'm not as tough as I think I am.' But the fear about women in combat, in my view, was based on genuine concern for their well being. And that has not been resolved yet. There are still significant restrictions on assignment of women to duties that would bring them directly into combat. That, in turn, means some artificial limits on what specialities and positions women can occupy."

On the other hand, Powe notes, women have come a long way in twenty years in the military services. The barriers to full equality are now relatively limited. For example, women can serve on U.S. Navy surface combat ships, but not in submarines. They can fly fighter aircraft, but not in fighter units committed to combat; and they can pilot Army utility helicopters at the front, but not armed attack helicopters. "These are distinctions with insignificant real differences," in Powe's view. As he sees it, once women were serving in the Army as equals to men in almost all fields, remaining inappropriate barriers began to fall by their own illogic. More will follow as time passes and pressure from women continues.

And the comparison to the role of women in athletics and in the military is clear for Powe: once women like Micki King and Lyn St. James had forced themselves fully into the realm of sports, particularly in those activities which had been previously restricted to men (such as high speed auto racing), remaining barriers were harder and harder to sustain. From this perspective, while full equality has not yet been achieved, the distance to travel is far less than the one already covered.

When we think about entering the boys' club, it seems as if few routes could be more challenging than for a woman driver entering the world of professional auto racing. Unlike the military services, there is no sense of shared national purpose which focuses opinion on the issue, nor is there a body of law which covers every aspect of the profession. Neither are there laws about equality of opportunity which govern professional athletics. So, when Lyn St. James decided to become a race driver in 1973, she was an anomaly. And she was *not* received warmly. She says of her driving career: "My entire career, it has always been, 'Who's going to work with the girl driver? Who's going to work with this bitch?' Many male drivers have told me, 'I couldn't do what you do.'"

But St. James has a philosophy which applies to her sport and which we think can be applied for all women entering the boys' club: "You have to live by the rules. You have to play by the rules. You have to win by the rules. Then, when you win enough, you can change the rules."[1]

Still the rules can be hard to live by, and the changes come slowly. (And sometimes, as discussed in the last chapter, the rules are unacceptable and must be fought.) A healthy sense of humor is imperative for those entering the boys' club. Take, for example, the 1995 national championship women's bobsled race in Lake Placid. Co-author Michelle and her brakewoman Sharon Slader were among the teams entered, and on the morning of the race they arrived early at the bobsled shed eager to see which sleds had been allocated for the women's race. Their smiles momentarily turned to worried grimaces. But they told themselves everything would be okay. Most of the sleds were equally bad, with rusted and worn runners on them, so at least no one had a major advantage. No one that is except the team using shiny racing runners (lent to them by a male domestic driver). But Michelle and Sharon were still confident they could win.

Their first run down was a little rougher than they would have liked, and Michelle kept asking anyone who would listen why the sled had continued to bump the left wall. She was oversteering, she was told. Michelle knew she wasn't oversteering, but she wasn't experienced enough to know what the problem was. The problem, it turned out, was a broken right steering cable. The sled, it was determined belatedly, was unusable. So Michelle and Sharon loaded the sled onto a truck and took it back down the mountain to get another sled (while the race was still underway). Okay, they told themselves, this is not a problem. It's not as if another sled could be worse, right?

Wrong. A pile of faded red fiberglass and bolts held together by duct tape sat in the middle of the sled shed. The cowling (hood) of the sled was not completely bolted down. The words "Help Me" had been painted across the nose. The women exchanged silent glances. But there was no time to be afraid. They loaded the sled onto a truck and raced back up the mountain. Michelle and Sharon frantically duct-taped the cowling down as best they could, and pulled the sled to the starting gate.

This run was smoother, no bouncing off the left wall. But Michelle kept wondering, *"Why are my legs cold?"* As they rounded the finish curve, she discovered why. The cowling was completely unattached (duct tape cannot withstand G forces) and air had been streaming through a six-inch gap. But the tight finish curve caused the cowling to fly up like a car hood blinding the driver. Michelle finished the race, peering under the cowling through her feet, and hoping that the cowling wouldn't fly off and kill Sharon. It didn't, and they won the race.

While this story is fairly typical of the kind of equipment U.S. women bobsledders have had to use over the past three years, and we've learned to see the humor, we also wonder if Lyn St. James' pit crew would ever have allowed her to climb into a duct-taped 1980 Toyota Corolla for a race. We kind of doubt it.

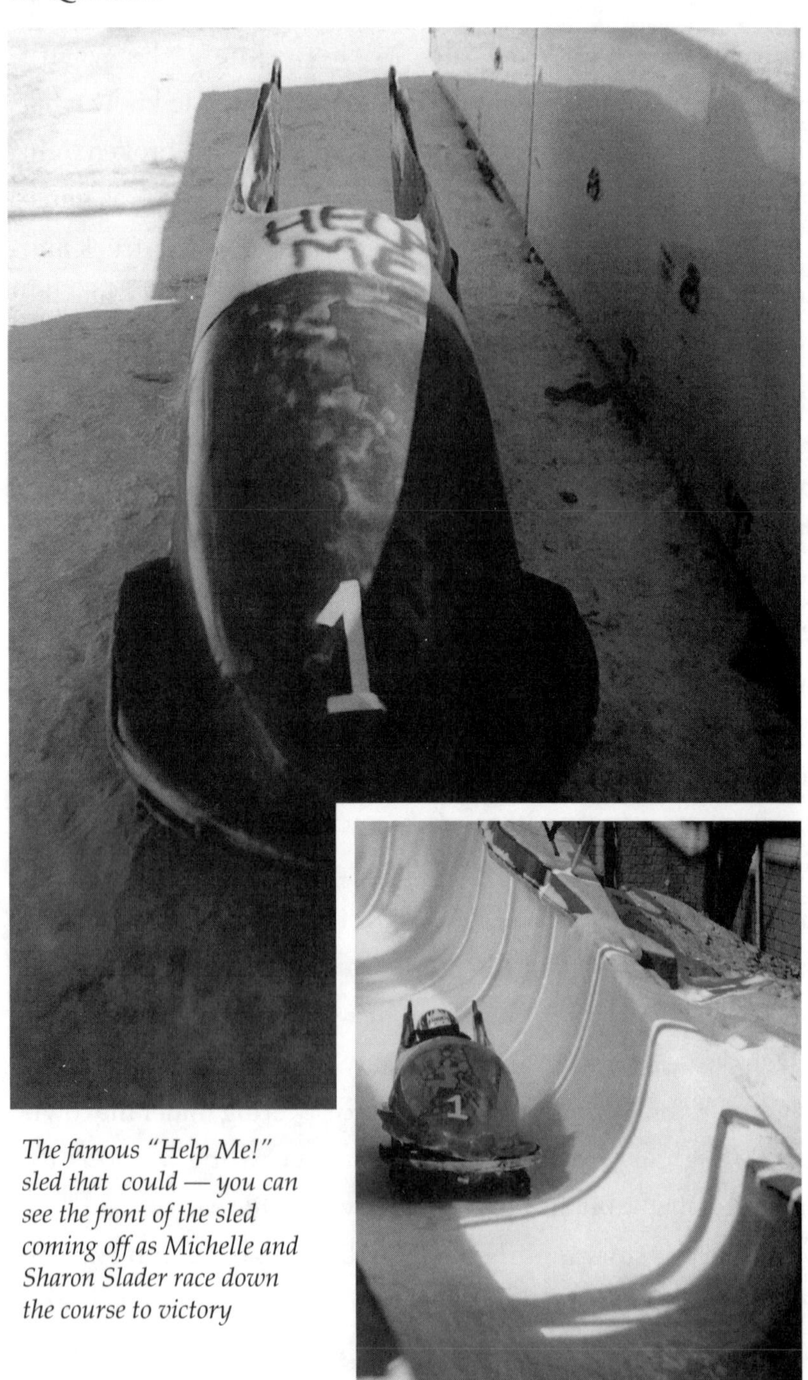

The famous "Help Me!" sled that could — you can see the front of the sled coming off as Michelle and Sharon Slader race down the course to victory

Still St. James, like us, like so many female athletes, had to prove herself over and over to men. Each time she demanded her right and proved her ability to race, she silenced a few more of those critics who said, "Who's going to work with this bitch?"

We wondered about such a visceral reaction by the other drivers. Were the men feeling threatened by this woman? At the time, by this *one* woman? We asked Micki King about her views since she has had successful careers as a gold-medal winning elite athlete (1972 Olympic Games, springboard diving), a military officer (retired Air Force colonel), a diving coach, and also has been a leader in advancing the rights of women athletes. "Certainly," she says, "I can understand that people would be threatened by an unknown breaking into their world. For me, it was quite different. I had luck getting into the boys' club, as you say, because I had credentials (her gold medal)."

But there were barriers of her own to break down. While coaching at the Air Force Academy, King became the first woman ever to coach a man to an NCAA championship in any sport. She also was named NCAA Division II Coach of the Year three times and coached 11 All-Americans, including two women cadets who won three national titles between them. But she says the only real discrimination she experienced was from reporters who wondered how she would coach the male cadets differently because she was a woman. Frustrated by the repeated questions, King finally told a reporter, "Well, first I'm going to cut out the locker room talks since I'm not allowed in, then I think I'll paint the diving board pink with a pink trim around the pool." She made her point.

Sue Blazejewski, former sports reporter for *The Miami Herald* and current bobsledder, has a stronger opinion as to why men would be intimidated. "If we're talking about women on the equal playing field with men, it's about ego. It is an ego threat to the man because what if the woman succeeds? It might just mean [he's] not as good, not as tough, as [he] thought. Whether true or not, it is very intimidating."

One of the most intimidating places for women to "invade" is the men's locker room, particularly given the discomfort both sexes feel with too much skin or too much physical contact. (Marc Powe, who is a pretty liberated guy, still shudders over the fact that his physical examination upon retirement from the Army was administered by a woman doctor. "Turn your head and cough. Hmm. How long have you had this hernia?" Arghhh!!!)

There is no doubt in the minds of some sports reporters that men feel threatened when women enter that bastion, the locker room. Julie Tache, reporter for 510-AM Sports Radio in Charlotte, North Carolina, says that when she asked some NFL players if her presence in the locker room bothered them, the answer was *yes*. "Most said they would feel more comfortable if I weren't there, but acknowledged I had a right to be there," Tache says. "Even though they realize this, it doesn't change how tense or self-conscious those same players feel when I am around, something few male reporters may experience." One outcome, Tache notes, is that if two reporters, one male and one female, ask the same question, they may get different answers, "especially depending on where they ask it."[2]

On the other hand, there may be real benefits in having the two different perspectives provided by men and women reporters, says Lisa Winston of *Baseball Weekly*. She identifies two major differences in the way she covers issues from her male colleagues: "One is that I don't reduce the player to a set of stats. The other is that I'm always polite and respectful to the player I'm interviewing."[3] Winston says that she is amazed at the brazen way some male reporters simply demand that the athlete instantly meet the reporter's need for an interview. She wonders if this is a basic difference between the style of men and women, or if it is peculiar to the milleau of sports.

We believe that there is a stylistic difference between men and women in all domains that has to do with empathy and cooperation. In essence, we think that women see things in terms of the need for cooperation in almost all cases, whereas men more frequently see things competitively. That is not to say that men cannot pull together; obviously, they do. And women, through the medium of sports among others, have learned from their male colleagues more about competitiveness and assertiveness. Nonetheless, we like being women and enjoy greatly the kind of cooperation we are experiencing. And we think that men could learn something from us on this topic.

But why, some might ask, *would you want to enter the men's domain — that crusty world of sports journalism and its associated, symbiotic relationship with the jocks?* We're talking real jocks in real jocks. *Leave well enough alone*, some might say.

No one knows that better than former *Washington Post* sports reporter Christine Brennan. Brennan had made herself a regular in the locker room of the Washington Redskins. One day while conducting an interview, she heard "Hey, Christine!" She turned to see about ten Redskins, wrapped in towels or already clothed huddled together in the middle of the locker room. "They parted like the Red Sea," she recalls, "to reveal [strength coach] Dan Reiley standing totally naked," wearing nothing but a huge grin.

"I said, 'Uh huh, that's nice' and turned back to my guy. His eyes were huge and I just looked at him as if to say, 'Okaaay, we're going to continue this interview now.'"

When we asked Brennan about breaking into the boys' club, she was very positive. Sure, she acknowledges, there have been incidents. "I'm not going to sugarcoat it. But there have been incidents with male reporters as well. Think about this: there are about 1,000 female reporters covering sports today. Just tonight, there will be about 50 female reporters in locker rooms across the country." Brennan runs over the questions she is most often asked.

Should women be in locker rooms?

"That's like asking if women should be allowed to vote! It is very *passe*. We're here. Deal with it."

Yeah, but don't you get embarrassed walking into men's locker rooms?

"I say, 'Look, I chose this job.' Of course, I can. Does anyone ever ask a doctor about seeing naked bodies? It's my job. And going into a locker room is part of it. It's like they say, to be a female reporter you have to be a little deaf and a little blind."

The Fabulous Sports Babe agrees. "I knew what I was getting into," she says. "If you get into this business and don't know what you're in for, you'll figure it out the second day." Or, you won't be back.

Tache sees it this way: "The best days are still the ones where someone calls the media 'guys,' and good or bad, I'm just like everyone else in the room."

Cris Dolan of ABC has this to say: "I remember when I was a child in the women's locker room at a country club, hearing women say they had to ask for their husband's permission. I remember thinking how great it was to be the husband. They had friends and did whatever they wanted. So I think I chose a career path that allowed me to be like the men."

A graduate (with a Ph.D.) of MIT, elite skeleton athlete, and director of Operations and Technology for ABC On-Line, Dolan says, "I remember thinking it would be better to be a man than a woman. I thought the roles of men were so much more interesting."

Having carved her own niche into the system, Dolan would be the first to tell you that women's "roles" are not less interesting, but at the time, as a child, entering the boys' club seemed like a way to salvation. Now, so many women have begun carving their niches into the system — such as the new female referees in the National Basketball Association — that women are beginning to be allowed to be both women and "the guys."

Being one of the guys in the guy's world can be very helpful, but also frustrating. But Jamie Humphrey, one of about 400 women of the 4,000 students at the U.S. Naval Academy in Annapolis, Maryland, dukes it out with the best of them. Literally.

Humphrey is a junior at a school that requires a heavy courseload, imposes strict discipline, and demands difficult physical work-out regimens. The Academy maintains that all candidates must take a physical education class every semester. And there are no exceptions for the women. They must run, lift, swim, and train just like the men — even when that includes boxing and wrestling. So while Humphrey bobs, weaves and yes, punches, she remains philosophical. "If this is going to be a gender-neutral Navy, we all ought to be on equal ground and we ought to get the same training. So, I'm glad we're doing it," Humphrey says.

For Humphrey, being considered "one of the guys," frees her from being labeled. "When you get here, first impressions are very important. You get labeled real fast." With a male-to-female ratio of 10-to-1, it is important not to stand out as a female. Humphrey has settled herself in nicely with the boys. But, she explains, it can be hard.

"We have a lot of female leadership because there are a lot of [women] seniors. Because we are a minority of the brigade, a lot of the guys resent the women's leadership roles. They say [the women] got it because of the equal opportunity laws, not because they earned it."

"Did they?" we wanted to know.

"Well, I don't personally know all of them but, yes, they earned it. The ones I know I feel are qualified and, at the very least, equal to any of the men."

But to defend them too much would only place her in that precarious female category again. It is something she is still trying to figure out. She enjoys being a female, wishes she could date, but is keenly aware of confusing her worlds. As it is, her undergarments have caused enough problems.

As freshmen, cadets are led through a six-week bootcamp in which they must learn the ropes of the Academy. That includes learning how to keep a room tidy, making beds, folding laundry. Squad leaders are in charge of groups of 12 cadets, two of whom are usually female.

It is the duty of the squad leaders to inspect rooms and to impose discipline, which often translates into throwing items around, yelling, and forever burning the cadet's mistake into his or her brain. A misplaced shoe polish bottle can easily be thrown across the room or used to draw all over something. But when the stern leaders came into then-freshman Humphrey's room and found an out-of-place tampon box, they were reduced to blushing teenaged boys. They managed to say, "Uh, you really need to move that."

"Move what, sir?"

"*That*," pointing awkwardly at the tampon box.

Her underwear were even more disconcerting. "They have a certain way you're supposed to fold your underwear," Humprey explains, "but the men don't know how to handle women's underwear."

Rather than tossing the improperly folded garments about the room, the squad leader sheepishly told Humphrey, "Uh,. . . you need to fix. . . that."

There is that female thing that is still so frightening to the male population. For example, Humphrey says, squad leaders, also called "detailers," have been instructed that if ever a female cadet says she has to go to the bathroom, *they must let her go*! No questions asked; after all, it might be *that* time of the month. During one five-mile run, Humphrey realized she really had to go to the bathroom. Now, she easily concedes, if a male cadet had to go he would either be forced to hold it or "go in the bushes," depending on the detailer's mood.

"I said, 'Sir, I reallllllly have to go.'" Without question, her detailer ran to the bathroom with her. "It's one of the ways guys are really discriminated against."

But these ways will continue until men learn to deal with women. The simplest things can be made difficult. Marine Major Ann Crittenden told us that she has learned at medal/promotion ceremonies to simply put her hand out and say, "Here, let me help you, sir," thereby relieving male officers of the apparently incapacitatingly embarrassing duty of pinning a medal on her chest.

Perhaps there is something to the power of the "female thing." Another interviewee suggested a funny way women could single-handedly fight crime. Imagine that a woman is alone in a dark alley. A mugger — a really, really big menacing-looking guy — approaches her. Suddenly, she pulls out a tampon, and not just the regular/slender style, but the super size. She waves it in his face, as he shields his eyes in terror.

"Back off, buddy! I don't want to have to use this, but I will!"

"Ahhhh!" he runs off, arms flailing in the air.

Now, if we could just funnel *that* power. . . .

Seriously, though, entering the boys' club can be confusing for a lot of women. Role models can be hard to find, in and out of the sports world. But as more and more women like Brennan and Donnellan break into the world of sports media, as more women break into all boys' clubs, whether sports or military or corporate America, media-encouraged stereotypes will fall apart, and more and more women will be allowed to "belong."

Women like Humphrey blaze trails of their own, not only as naval cadets and serious students, but in teaching *men* how to deal with *women*. We hope we are doing this in bobsledding as well. And, for this reason alone, the entry of women into the boys' club can only make all of its members better, stronger, wiser. After all, we should all belong to the same club, no exclusionary rules.

As Lt. Gen. Carol Mutter, U.S. Marine Corps, says: "When you act like you belong, you are treated that way. If you act like you're breaking a barrier, or act too tentative or nonassertive, you can be treated negatively. So I have always acted like I belonged." And belong she does.

Chapter Ten

You've Come a Long Way, Baby!

At the announcement of Muffin Spencer-Devlin's "coming out," LPGA commissioner Jim Ritt had this to say: "I know there are still individuals who have problems with diversity, but we've come so far as a society that I don't see this as a topic that really moves people." Maybe not, but to have one of the Ladies Professional Golf Tournament's biggest players come out of the closet and publicly admit her sexual preference did two things for women in sports: it further fueled stereotypes about female athletes ("Yup, uh huh, I knew it!") and, at the same time, it elevated us to a new freedom from stereotypes.

History despite its wrenching pain
Cannot be unlived, but if faced
With courage, need not be lived again.
— Maya Angelou

There is a theory in sports psychology that women athletes may have more masculine traits and behaviors than women who are not athletes. Perhaps this is because competitiveness is still considered a masculine trait in our society. But whatever the reasoning, the result is the same: many female athletes are labeled butch, lesbian, man-wanna-be's, deviant. Nevermind that there is no evidence that there is a higher percentage of lesbians in sports than in society as a whole. (And nevermind, that it shouldn't matter, anyway.) These labels are intended as insults, to discourage women from being "un-feminine" and, perhaps, to send messages to stop challenging men. It may sound like a ridiculous ploy, but it works.

Adolescent girls regularly drop out of sports rather than endure the taunts. And competitive athletes spend far too much time defending themselves against allegations about sexual orientation, avoiding or denying, when attention should be focused on their sports. Great athletes like Billie Jean King and Martina Navratilova had as much media time devoted to their sexual preferences as to their amazing athletic abilities and legacies. Just as mothers are questioned about their dedication to their sports and the implied cost to their children, many women are suspect just for loving sports. In fact, Navratilova says she is thankful no one knew she was gay when she first came to the United States at the age of 18. Had people known, she admits, she wouldn't be who she is today.

And the innuendos are just as difficult for straight athletes, who don't want to be labeled gay. U.S. softball gold medalist Dot Richardson might not have been who she is today if she had listened to such labels. She admits it was hard sometimes rising above the rumors. "I kept wondering, 'Why do I have to put up with this? Why does this keep popping up? What is wrong with me?'" She says many of her friends in high school quit sports because of the innuendos, and she understands why they quit.

"I believe that the stereotyping of female athletes as lesbians has been one of the biggest hindrances to the development of women in sports," she says.[1] How many girls and women might have been athletic standouts, might have been gold medalists, might have developed true self-confidence, if they hadn't let others' opinions dictate their lives and cause them to quit sports?

The females who do rise above the fray may accomplish great things, but they also pay a price. Allie Sizler, a high school standout basketball player, has been accused of being a lesbian. Sizler's mother told us, "Whatever Allie felt was okay with her father and me, but she said, 'Mom, I like boys.' I thought, 'Okay,' but that really didn't matter. It was what was happening at school."

What was happening at school was a group of athletes, intimidated by Allie's athletic prowess, decided that she must be gay. No one girl could be that dedicated, that focused, that good and be "normal." In fact, an ex-boyfriend started the rumor. Playing second fiddle to Allie's true passion — sports — was more than his adolescent ego could handle. *There had to be something wrong with Allie.*

Julie Croteau was routinely accused of wanting to be a man because she coached NCAA Division I baseball, accused of "getting off on the power of yelling at men." At the very least, such behavior was not considered "feminine."

Beyond appearance and femininity, there is also a standard — a double standard — for feminine behavior. Sports psychologist Pat Bach points to Nancy Kerrigan, "whose poor behavior in winning the silver medal in the 1994 Olympics did not meet expectations for proper behavior," and who was roundly criticized by media, sponsors, and the public. But Bach wonders, "If a man had behaved so poorly, would sponsors have rejected him, too?" The Phoenix Suns' superstar Charles Barkley is notorious for misbehaving, yet he has giant endorsement contracts. It is, after all, part of his charm. Similarly, the Chicago Bulls' Dennis Rodman has been enriched by his bad-boy image. And while professional baseball, football, and hockey players continue to behave badly on and off the playing fields, to spit in the face of or headbutt officials, to abuse drugs and alcohol, and to commit assault and spousal abuse, we continue to support and celebrate them. Simply put, Kerrigan didn't act nicely for a woman. Her behavior was out of the norm for "proper feminine behavior."

Babe Didrikson-Zaharias gloated to reporters that she was the best; she predicted before meets how she would fare (always the best); she told knee-slapping jokes to the boys in the press-room. They loved her. Her fellow competitors were not so gracious. How could she act that way? Mothers began to warn their daughters away from sports, saying "You don't want to be like Babe."

The double standard against women actually works more than one way. Not only are women held to a standard of behavior higher than men's (i.e., "proper feminine behavior"), but they also are held to a lower standard of behavior. "The media like to portray female athletes as catty," says Hilliard. Take the highly-publicized rift between Gwen Torrence and Gail Devers, or the challenge issued to three-time Olympian Janet Evans by 15-year-old Brook Bennett, saying, "She's scared." But there were no "cat fights." Instead, when the media-proclaimed "fastest woman," Gwen Torrence, took the bronze medal in the 100 meters, she came out on to the track, grabbed gold-medal-winner Gail Devers' hand and led her for her victory lap. Torrence told us, "A lot of people were cheering for me to take a lap because it was my hometown, but I didn't want to disrespect Gail. I felt in my heart that the right thing to do was to run with the champion." And Janet Evans was gracious before and after the Games, making it clear that she would not be dragged into any war of words.

But that portrayal of "cattiness" is a fairly widely-held misconception. We ran across many opinions that women (and therefore female athletes) are "back-stabbing, manipulative, petty"; that you can't have a group of women together without having "cat fights." This last point is particularly interesting because while female athletes tend to bond with each other more closely than male athletes do, we are also more deeply disappointed when we feel a teammate has let us, or the team, down. This "pettiness" that many seem to view as a female trait is, in fact, the absence of a socialized male trait. Too many girls do not learn the written and unwritten rules about sports, about how to be competitive on the field and friends off the field.

But none of the comments about women being unable to get along in groups surprised sports psychologist Coleen Hacker. "Society or the dominant culture would prefer that women not participate in one-on-one sports," Hacker says, adding that gymnastics, golf, and figure skating are very popular for that reason. "Even tennis, because the opponents are separated by a net." Ironically, it was a tennis match — that most famous first battle of the sexes between Billie Jean King and former tennis champ Bobby Riggs — that finally allowed women to take their rightful place in the sports world and begin to knock down some stereotypical boundaries. (King beat Riggs, 6-4, 6-3, 6-3.) Stereotypes aside, the reality is that women do get along in teams. What we have seen in women's team sports is very different from the men's teams. And even those male team members are inclined to agree that there is a kind of easiness, friendship, and camaraderie among the women that the men don't usually share.

During the 1996-97 U.S. Bobsled Nationals, two women had come late to the camp and tested three days later than the rest of us. Those of us who had already taken the six-item test (30-, 60-, and 100-meter dash, five hops, vertical jump, and shot put throw) and made the points, spent the morning on sled-pushing drills while the two late-comers ran their 30-meter, 60-meter, and 100-meter dashes. At lunch break, we saw the women walking into the gymnasium to take the remaining three events.

Just that morning, we had learned that one of the women, Liz, was pregnant with her second child. Five months pregnant, to be exact. Many of us were nervous for her. Five months is pretty far along to effectively run, hop, leap, and throw. We were all worried about how well she would do. Then, one of those things that you hear about in the best-of-sports-stories happened. Instead of counting Liz out, figuring she was one less competitor, the large majority of the women who attended the nationals, including women who had not met Liz before this day, went into the gymnasium to cheer her on. She needed the points and we wanted them for her.

While we all nibbled on our chocolate chip cookies and milk (one of our favorite rewards for jobs well done), we cheered Liz through her vertical leap and shot put. Then, we overheard a testing official say she needed to hop 12 meters. She had already hopped twice and had only hit 10.65 meters. Later it would be funny, later we would be teased by the male bobsledders: one by one, all the women put down their chocolate chip cookies and concentrated on Liz. As one male slider put it, "Now that's love when eight women all stop eating their chocolate chip cookies at the same time!"

Liz couldn't hit 12 meters — not five months pregnant. We all cheered and yelled, but in the end 10.65 would be her best. And while Liz anxiously paced the floor, we all gathered around the testing official. A few male bobsledders watched from afar.

"I get 429," one teammate said, doing the math in her head.

Liz needed to score 425 to make the team, and the testing official had tallied her score as 419. Another woman nodded, "Yeah, I get 429, too."

After several recounts, it was discovered the tester had miscalculated. And before he could even make it official, the gymnasium reverberated with whoops of joy. Liz was hugged from all sides and she hugged back hard, and there were many, many tears. Our teammate had felt our support, our concern. She had made the points just as much for us as she did for herself. We were all so proud.

Looking through the windows of the gym were three male sliders, grinning and shaking their heads. In the men's camp, the feeling is that every man out is one less guy between me and the 'A' team. But here was this group of women bobsledders hugging and whooping, the prized chocolate chip cookies forgotten. We took the teasing and felt a little bit sorry for the men for whom group support was so foreign. Forget what you read in the papers, boys; *this* is what women's sports are about!

And there are also many wonderful stories of camaraderie between female and male athletes. Karen Bye of the U.S. women's hockey team tells about growing up playing hockey as the only girl on the team. Not only did she become a full-fledged team member in the eyes of her teammates, she was also like a sister to many of them. "At one of our games in high school, the opposing team asked which number the girl was. They told them I was number 23. Number 23 was the biggest guy on our team [and he] had a beard."

The guys had fun with Bye, and there were laughs, but always they protected her. Since there were some other players who set out to "hurt" her, Bye's own teammates would help Bye disguise who she was. She put only her initials on the team roster, so parents and players from other teams would not know who she was. "My hair was real short. A lot of the guys on my team had longer hair than I did."

Record-setting race car driver Lyn St. James, spokesperson for the Women's Sports Foundation and Ford Motor Company, television commentator and author, told us about the very special connection she has with her pit crew, not the usual driver-pit crew relationship. Much to the frustration of the all-male crew, St. James is hopelessly modest. There were many times when St. James performed well in a race but questioned her ranking, not believing she had "earned" her ratings.

St. James recalls a particular competition, the Kelly Services Races, at which the top women racers were to be honored. Following the race, the number one woman driver would receive an award during a ceremony before the large audience. As always, St. James had underestimated her talents: she had expected to place fifth but, to her surprise, she had won! She also had started her period.

Wearing her white racing suit, she pulled into the pit and politely refused to get out of the car. While dozens of people raced into the pit area, and her own crew yelled at her to get out, St. James shook her head. "Nope. I'm not getting out." Believing St. James to be playing the humble role again, the crew chief stuck his head into the car and began pulling her out. St. James grabbed

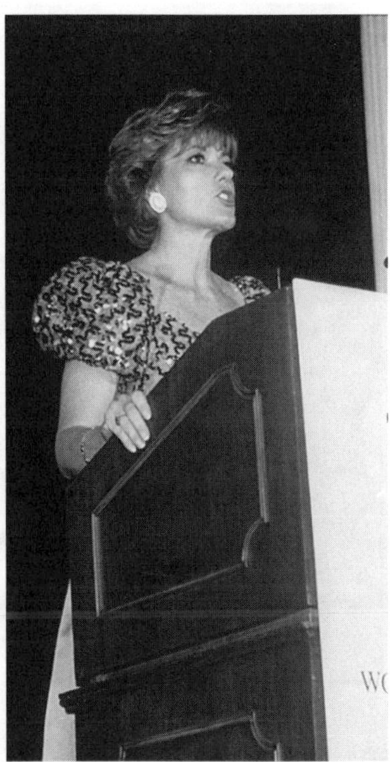

Lyn St. James is a leader on and away from the track

Rachael Myllymaki

his head and turned it so he could see that her white racing suit was soaked with menstrual blood. "He said only three words," St. James remembers. "'Oh, my God!'"

Immediately, he rallied the crew and they pushed St. James' car out of the pit area, and smuggled her into the locker room. Even as the sponsors were calling her name, her crew protected her from the crowds. Not another word was ever said about that incident, but her crew gave her a present — a black racing suit.

As far as rodeo rider Rachael Myllymaki is concerned, she is just one of the cowboys. As barrel racers, the women ride just before the bull riders. Myllymaki and the other women mill around the alley after the horses are warmed up, waiting for their time slot. But Myllymaki has learned to keep an eye out as it is not unusual for some of the cowboys to push the bridle off of one of the horse's ears. It has happened that she has jumped on her horse, ridden out to the arena, and the bridle has simply slipped off, making control of the horse impossible.

Why would they do that?

"Because they're butts," she laughs. Practical joking, we learned, is common practice on the rodeo circuit and a sign of acceptance. Having a joke played on you means you are considered one of the boys — a high compliment. And being accepted by the boys can be more than a good feeling. It is also essential for smooth sailing in a sport like rodeo which involves moving heavy equipment and animals.

That sort of cooperation is also essential in the sport of bobsledding, where teams must work as units to move 450-pound sleds and lift them in and out of trucks. And our bobsledding brothers have begun helping us move and repair sleds, occasionally lending us equipment or walking the tracks with us. They have stolen *the last brownie in the whole cafeteria* off our trays. (They say they are watching our weight for us. Isn't that nice? Although they do bring us candy when we're injured in crashes.)

We have been the female version of the Jamaican bobsled team: starting with nothing and leading each other blindly through the maze of a new sport. But along the way, despite the obstacles, we've encountered some tremendous gestures. In international competition, with our rented and dented sleds and no coach, the British and Canadians have loaned us equipment. The German coaches have put their arms around us, helped us through competitions, visited us in the hospital, and given us a tour of what was once East Germany. British and Canadian coaches have walked the tracks with us. The Swiss have translated for us, and the Swiss and Canadians have literally climbed into our sleds to make adjustments for us. And that kind of support is not unique to bobsledding. Ski jumper Karla Keck has had similar experiences while training in Europe.

Women are able to bring that spirit of cooperation and camaraderie to sports, and bring out those qualities in others around them. For example, our bobsledding brothers are not as generous with each other as they are with us. They have admitted that the women broke the tension that always hung over the training center and kept them apart; they enjoy our company. As Joseph Taylor, sales and marketing director of the lacrosse and soccer equipment company Brine, Inc., says, "Women tend to be more able to draw the fun out of sports. They have a better appreciation for what sports mean."

That appreciation was demonstrated during a women's World Cup soccer game between the United States and Italy. An Italian player was hurt while the U.S. had possession of the ball, so the referee could not call time-out. But it was clear that the player was hurt, so a U.S. player passed the ball to an Italian player, giving the Italians possession and allowing the referee to call time-out. After the player was attended to, play resumed with a throw-in by the Italians. The Italian player with the ball returned the earlier favor by throwing the ball directly to an American defender, thus giving the U.S. possession again.

How we do love to watch women play sports!

During the pre-Olympic show for the Centennial Games, while some of the more outgoing athletes mugged for cameras and interviews, U.S. diver Becky Rheul hung back. Terribly shy, she withdrew from all the excitement. Rheul's mother, Clair, was concerned that Rheul would miss some great opportunities and a lot of fun if she didn't get into the action. Fellow diver Mary

Ellen Clark took care of that. She continually pulled Rheul to the front saying, "C'mon, Beck!"

Clair Rheul told us, "There were times when Becky was just standing there and someone would ask Mary Ellen something, like 'What are you going to do?' and Mary Ellen would say, 'Well, I think Becky. . . .' She was great about pulling Becky into everything, including her. That really meant a lot to us."

Another of the many women's teams known in the Olympic circles for its camaraderie is the U.S. women's hockey team. Just like their soccer sisters, when the assistant coach of the women's hockey team brought her baby along for the World Cup tour, each female hockey player grabbed something of the baby's (a bag of food, formula, diapers) along with her own possessions. In fact, as the team hustled to make a plane they were close to missing, Karen Bye scooped up the baby boy and sprinted through the airport. No one thought any differently about carrying the baby and baby things than they did about hustling their hockey equipment. They were a package deal. All for one and one for all.

Coach Tara VanDerveer of the U.S. women's basketball team said the finale of the Olympic games, winning the gold medal, was the happiest and saddest day of her life. While she called her athletes "warriors ready for battle," they were also "family." Together, all the women worked, trained, and dreamed together. They traveled far, seeking personal goals and working together to gain the attention and respect they so greatly deserved.

Most female athletes understand VanDerveer's feeling. We have felt the frustration of being treated as jokes, called wanna-be's, and told plainly that we are "wasting our time." While the negativity itself has been draining, it has also served to pull women together. We have seen and been encouraged by women in our own and in other sports, women in other times, all fighting for their sports, for approval, and for acceptance.

But imagine this. You are in the Olympic Games. You are standing as the anchor for the women's 4x100 relay. Billions of people are watching you on television, thousands are watching you from the stands. You're jiggling your arms and legs, trying to keep the muscles loose and warm. You're rolling your head from side to side. Your heart is pounding. You are running over the race in your mind, how you will take the baton, take off. The gun goes off! The race is on. . . then, "Pssst! Your tampon string is showing!"

"What?"

Gwen Torrence turned to face a woman named Pauline Davis from Team Bahamas. Davis was pointing down to Torrence's shorts.

"Your tampon string," she repeated.

Mortified, Torrence tried to tuck it back inside the seam of her outfit. The baton was passed off to the second leg. Davis was shaking her head at Torrence. It was still showing.

Davis, then, actually crossed over her line into Torrence's lane to help. Imagine being in the middle of perhaps the biggest event of your life, and here are Torrence and Davis huddled together in Torrence's lane, fixing a tampon string.

"It was so embarrassing," Torrence says. "I don't know why I was so embarrassed, but I couldn't help it. And everyone was saying, 'Why are those girls standing together? What are they doing?'"

By the time the third leg was coming around for Torrence, Torrence said, "Oh, forget it!" She got the baton, took off, and won the gold for the U.S. Interestingly, the Bahamian team won the silver, making it the first time in the Bahamas' history that women have medaled in any sport.

Later, reporters asked Torrence what she and Davis were talking about. Imagine two women, under these conditions, bonding in some "female way." Torrence laughs, "I told them, 'It was a female thing.'"

Upon reflection, it appears to us that those who imagine that girls or women as a group are petty or back-stabbing do not know much about women athletes. They have not experienced the exasperating, exciting, exhausting, exhilarating world of women's sport. We are sure that those who do not believe women can be happy in large competitive groups simply have not cried, sweated, and laughed together as hard as we have. Indeed, VanDerveer said that the end of the Olympic quest for her basketball team was like losing her family. Here is the point: women, at least in team sports, must be close to be successful. We must stick together individually to make progress collectively.

When Mary Ellen Clark prepared for what would be her last Olympic Games, the competition was tough. She knew it. She was recovering from vertigo, diving against girls half her age, including U.S. diver Becky Rheul. But instead of keeping all her experience and all her secrets to herself, Clark drew Rheul in. For Rheul, a first-time Olympian, it was an especially nerve-racking time. Rather than capitalize on that, Clark (Rheul's roommate at the Games) offered her advice about the competition and the audience. She warned Rheul not to let the crowd intimidate her, but rather, "Let the sounds be a blanket of warmth to soothe you." Rheul would later tell her mother that this advice worked. And anyone who watched the 1996 Games and the women's diving competition probably asked the question we did whenever Rheul stood on the diving platform: *why is she smiling?*

What could possibly be so amusing at this point in her life? Didn't she have other things to think about, like not killing herself? But Rheul was taking Clark's advice to heart. She was doing what she loved most in life and the cheers of the home crowd only reminded her of that.

Clair Rheul says of Clark, "She was willing to take the time to pass on her wisdom and share her experience. We really appreciate that and, hopefully, Becky will do the same at her next Olympics.

"This is what we need to keep good athletes going, to keep the cycle going. We are all very much a family. Both Becky and Mary Ellen come from large families, so during the Olympics we all sat together, and even Mary Ellen's parents told us it felt like we were one family. We were."

In fact, with the Games long over, both divers continue to send each other notes and gifts.

As trainer Radu says, when we learn to work together as a watch, all of us acting as perfect little pieces for the greater whole, then, we work well together.

In May 1994, bobsledder Jill Bakken had an enormous amount of school work to plow through. School officials had not been happy that she had to attend a camp in May, just weeks before her final examinations and graduation from high school.

All week we had trained, sweated, and collapsed onto our beds from sheer exhaustion. It was near the end of the week and Jill had completed only half of her schoolwork. Her team pitched in, helping set up essay questions to test her. We each studied certain subjects so that we could quiz her. While one teammate took physics, another took math, and another took history.

It was early Sunday morning and Alex sat alone in the cafeteria writing some test questions for Jill. Having spent all night brushing up on her post-WWII history, Alex was preparing some tough questions when a hand reached over her shoulder. A handmade card dropped onto the open book, and the unseen messenger was gone. A plain white piece of paper, folded in half, had been drawn on by Jill's loving hands. Little baby ducks, flowers, and wildlife decorated the cover. Inside was a very tender message wishing Alex a "Happy Mothers Day!"

It was Alex's first Mother's Day card ever. It was the second time she had ever been away from Kerri, then only eleven months old. Of course, the tears came and Alex turned in her seat to see if Jill was nearby. Standing outside of the cafeteria, Jill was pressed against the glass, watching Alex.

A sound from the other side of the cafeteria caught Alex's attention and she turned to see FIBT official Joey Kilburn, who had been watching the entire exchange take place. He pretended to wipe a tear away from his cheek. He was not making fun. Clearly, he too was deeply moved by this silent exchange of affection. It was not long after that that Kilburn told us how struck he was by the kinship shared by the women sledders.

Whatever our social or sexual preferences, we are all women — and can be women and athletes. One does not suffer because of the other; in fact, each can be improved by the other.

Two years later, as we neared the end of our week at the 1996 Nationals, all the women had made their points, and it did become woman against woman. The next cut-off for making the team was qualifying in the top eight in the sled push competition. As we all sat at the top of the hill, stretching, each in our own thoughts, newcomer Jean Racine climbed the hill for her turn. As she climbed, she came into view of Chrissy, a competing driver.

"Hi, sweetie," Jean said.

"Hi, cupcake," Chrissy responded.

Yep, it was getting pretty cut-throat out here at competition time.

Chapter Eleven

The Quietest of Storms

> *I am just a person trapped inside a woman's body.*
> —Elaine Boosler

Women's sports history has such a large archive of role models, of pioneers, to whom we should give credit and thanks and from whom we can learn. Courageous, determined athletes who have dared to cross the line. Women who have dared to venture into no-woman's land. Women who have dared to perform dangerous, risky feats that few men would dare attempt.

In 1925, for example, a young American woman named Gertrude Ederle attempted to swim the English Channel. Only 18 years old, she had already broken world records, had an Olympic gold medal, and held 250 swimming records. However, the weather and frigid water temperatures of the Channel were too much for her on that day, and she was forced to quit after nine hours in the water.

As word spread that this "little girl" had attempted such a feat, *The New York Daily News* sponsored Ederle, offering her $5,000 to attempt the swim again and $7,500 if she succeeded.

They even drafted her to be a correspondent and write her own story. "I want to be the first woman to swim from France to England. I know a woman can do it," she insisted.

As she prepared for her second attempt in 1926, and as her celebrity status rose, she became the topic of a very heated debate. Was she the symbol of a new, healthy woman willing to take on risks, striking out on her own? Or was she an example of the weaker sex over-reaching? Surely, some reasoned, her failure would only prove the frailities of her sex.

Coated with three layers of grease, the top coat being a kind of thick car axle grease for insulation, Ederle plunged into the icy waters, setting out toward her goal. She swam behind a boat holding her father and sister and filled with reporters. Occasionally, people jumped into the water and swam beside her to keep her company. Her sister, father, and the reporters leaned over the side of the boat to sing her songs, entertaining and encouraging her along the way.

Sports historians estimate this kind of journey is perhaps one of the loneliest of the sports triumphs. Even with her supporters there, much of Ederle's time was spent in the darkness of the water, alone. Yet she was not alone. Ederle felt the weight of the world on her shoulders and recognized that many, many women were counting on her to complete this journey. Wall Street brokers wagered three-to-one against her, and one reporter with *The Daily News* proclaimed her actions were a reminder to us all that "females must forever remain the weaker sex."

The weather worsened and the winds picked up, making Ederle's strokes much more difficult. She was attacked twice by a Portuguese man-of-war that stung her horribly. But she told her family and coach, "I must keep going."

Fourteen hours and 34 minutes later, Ederle touched England's soil — a time that was one hour and fifty-nine minutes faster than that of any man who had swum the channel. Billed as "woman swimmer, champion of both sexes," Ederle traveled to New York for the United States' first-ever ticker-tape parade, and was greeted by a crowd of two million people. She did not lose her femininity because of her accomplishments.

Neither did Amelia Earhart. Earhart was the first woman to make a solo transcontinental round trip flight (in 1928), the first woman to fly across the Atlantic (also in 1928), and the first woman to fly solo across the Atlantic Ocean (in 1932), breaking down the stereotype that women were limited in their abilities. She was also greeted with ticker-tape parades. She won several flying awards in her lifetime, including the Distinguished Flying Cross.

There were no ticker-tape parades for Marcenia (Toni) Stone, who broke the gender barrier in baseball. She played second base for the Indianapolis Clowns of the Negro American League from 1953-1955, after having already played on men's semipro teams in San Francisco and New Orleans. After her professional baseball career ended, Stone continued to play in men's amateur leagues until she was 60 years old. But she got no official recognition, and is not included in any of the exhibits at the Negro Leagues Baseball Museum in Kansas City. Stone said in 1993, "I just loved the game. But they weren't ready for me. . . . But my heart was set. And I kept at it."[1]

These women first established the notion that females are physically capable of anything, and paved the way for women today. Often facing male-dominated fields with no mentors and few supporters, these women were more than pioneers. They were adventurers, exhibitionists, and test pilots for what was to come.

But many of the greatest role models in women's athletics had accomplishments outside the world of sports. The celebrity status of such women lent credibility to their causes.

Babe Didrikson-Zaharias was one such woman. Babe's athletic feats are well known, but not so well known is the fact that she became an advocate for cancer treatment at a time when the disease was not well known or understood. In 1953, at the height of her career, Babe was diagnosed with colon cancer and underwent an emergency colostomy. Three and a half months after the surgery, she returned to the LPGA tour, and the following year she won the US Women's Open by a record 12 strokes. After her victory, she said: "This should show people not to be afraid of cancer."

True to her nature, Babe hid nothing from the press or the people. She allowed the press to travel with her, keeping them apprised of all her ailments. Her openness was all the more remarkable because there was a real stigma attached to cancer patients in the 1950s. It was a disease many did not understand and, therefore, feared. Babe was the first person to campaign against the disease, stimulating a national fund-raising campaign which was led by President Dwight Eisenhower. In 1956, Babe lost her only fight. After her death, Eisenhower made a public tribute to her, saying, "Babe took on the kind of fight that inspires us all."

In fact, we were pleased to see in the *Sports Illustrated* poll that Mary Decker Slaney was one athlete who did not mention a male athlete as a role model. She wrote, "There have been so many great athletes, but I most admire Babe Didrikson-Zaharias."

Diver Pat McCormick established Pat's Chance, helping kids from disadvantaged backgrounds so that they may pursue higher education and business opportunities. McCormick saw to it that her athletic ability would help others and she has been rewarded in an unusual way. McCormick says she knows when she leaves this earth she will have accomplished what she set out to do. Diving was a glorious time for her, but through her physical ability, she also has been allowed an opportunity to help others. Beyond the physical benefits of sport, what a great sense of spiritual accomplishment McCormick can feel.

Bonnie Blair speaks and raises money for U.S. charities, and has created the Bonnie Blair Charitable Gift Fund, which supports a variety of causes, including cancer research (her brother Rob suffers from a malignant brain tumor) and child welfare. In 1996, the World Sports Humanitarian Hall of Fame gave her its Sports Humanitarian Award.

This chapter's title, "The Quietest of Storms," is actually dedicated to sprinter Wyomia Tyus. Tyus dedicated her last gold medal earned in the 4x400 meter relay at the 1968 Olympics to two fellow U.S. athletes who became overnight pariahs. During the 1968 Mexico City Games, as they stood on the medal stand, runners Tommie Smith and John Carlos raised their fists in the air as a silent protest to the treatment of African-Americans. It was a silent protest that got them expelled from the Olympic Village.

"All I did was win a track event. What they did lasted a lifetime," Tyus explains. Downplaying her gesture, and the fact that she grew up in a segregated school system, Tyus says simply that she adjusted to what came her way. Now, Tyus works with city kids in an outdoor program, taking them away from the city, trying to build self-esteem.

When asked if she considers herself a role model, Tyus laughs and says, "Only because people keep telling me I am." Again, she continues to minimize her contributions, naming others for credit. Then, she adds modestly, after some thought, "Maybe I am a quiet role model."

As her coach Ed Temple from Tennessee State says, Tyus is "one of the pioneers for women and blacks."

Elaine Cheris not only trains herself to be an Olympic fencer, but runs a school for her sport as well. She staunchly believes that sports help children socially. Of her girls, Cheris says, "They're less likely to walk off with the first boy who blinks at them. Girls and boys learn to work with each other. They train like brothers and sisters; they scream and cry together. There is a mutual respect." And, absolutely, Cheris does not allow the battle of the sexes to take place in her school. Not only does she forbid any form of "hazing," but she also demands that her students praise each other. "You beat him 15-0. Now," she will tell her charges, "go over and tell him he really made you reach. Tell him he really made you work hard."

Valerie Still plays so "little girls can dream"

Having written a book about fencing, Cheris offers not only her expertise as an athlete, but is a strong role model for people of all ages. She stresses the importance of pushing yourself to know your limits, always refusing to hear and be stifled by the negative. She always reminds her kids that winning comes from inside. And Cheris serves as a role model for those who have been told or have believed that age limited their successes and dreams. At 50, Cheris thinks nothing of her age, or the fact that so few athletes male or female continue to compete so long. And she ignores those who would remind her of it (in the negative sense). She says, "People will give you a thousand reasons to lose. They don't really want you to, but they just tell you all the reasons you can't [win]." Can't. A word she just hates to hear.

"Can't" is a word Lisa Fernandez also refuses to hear. As though the coach's words still burn in her ears ("You'll never be able to compete past sixteen."), Fernandez is determined to be a positive role model for young hopefuls. Two or three times a month, Fernandez offers softball clinics around the country. She gives inspirational talks, works with coaches, and remains an undaunted supporter of women's athletics. With a personal motto of "Never be satisfied," Fernandez continues to push all those around her to be the best they can be. What better role model?

"Can't" is a word Wilma Rudolph and Althea Gibson also refused to hear. And, of course, no list of pioneers in the world of sports would be complete without these two names. They stand as symbols of progress, not only for women, not only for African-Americans, but for all people. Both women came from very poor backgrounds, and both broke down barriers for women and for people of color. Today, they are remembered as women of tremendous talent, grace, sportsmanship, with the wills to be the best they could be.

And already at the age of 11, Danielle Lundy stands ready for the responsibility of role model. Not because she just might be the first African-American breaststroker to qualify for the U.S. Olympic swim team, but because she knows she serves as an inspiration to so many people.

Like Lundy, race car driver St. James is very modest, but ready to accept the responsibility. "If I really dig down, I can accept it," she says. "It's hard to understand why I would be considered a role model. I think of role models as people who do something you want to do and want to try — something accessible. So, I wrestle with that, but I hold it in high regard. I don't hold it like Charles Barkley."

St. James is a role model, and her actions on and off the race track attest to how seriously she takes that responsibility. In her 20 years of racing, St. James has set 31 national and international records, been named Indianapolis 500 Rookie-of-the-Year in 1992, and has competed in the Indy 500 every year since. She was the first solo woman driver to win a professional road race, the first woman to exceed 200 miles per hour on an oval track, and the first woman to compete full-time on the Indy circuit.

Off the track, St. James has established the Lyn St. James Foundation and Driver Development Program, the goal of which is to help new female race car drivers and business executives develop skills for winning, skills needed in racing and in living. She is also the author of a car maintenance manual for women.

St. James serves on the consumer advisory board for the Ford Motor Company and on the board of the Colorado Bullets, the first all-female professional baseball team. She is a past president of the Women's Sports Foundation. And she is an accomplished classical pianist and mother of a 12-year-old daughter.

How did this remarkable woman get into the male-dominated sport of racing? St. James says she had not really given it much thought until one evening in her junior year in high school. She went to watch some friends in a drag race. When they lost, St.

James complained, and someone said, "Okay, then, why don't you drive?" So she did, and she won.

When she told her mother what had happened, her mom said, "You did what?" St. James says she thinks that her mom is still waiting for her to get racing out of her system. But her mom also said, "If you're gonna do it, do it well."

Do it well. That's Tony Little's philosophy.

Little was a national bodybuilder until he was hit by a school bus in 1983. It changed his life, causing him to refocus everything he thought was important. He became a certified instructor, eventually creating his own medical advisory board, teaching millions of people every day the importance of nutritional and physical exercise. But his real impact has been his concern about today's youth.

It was Little who brought to our attention that only one state, Illinois, requires daily physical education in school. We were surprised and disappointed by this, although it offers yet one more explanation for the rise in obesity among children in this country. Little is very worried about the future and well-being of our children. Recently, Little was asked to attend a school assembly in southern Florida where he was to receive an award. When he stepped up to the microphone, he called out to the kids, ready to get them fired up. It is, after all, what Little does best. "How many of you want to be successful in the world?" he asked. To his disbelief, only about fifty percent of the kids answered him. "What is this?! They just sat there," he says. "It was one of the worst days of my life. I realized these kids don't care. They have all the stress of the world, but they don't have the dreams or support from their families like we had."

Little is more determined than ever to motivate young people, to make physical education a part of their lives, and he will talk to anyone who will listen.

With such caring, self-sacrificing people as examples, the Sameka Randalls and Tia Trents of the world may be our up-and-coming role models. Tia's mother, Cheryl, told us that one day she walked into the kitchen to hear Tia chastising a friend over the phone. Tia told her friend not to call her or talk to her until she improved her grades. The disgusted Tia then explained to her mother that while she would miss her friend, she wasn't going to let her hang around as long as she was "acting stupid." Tia has a definite agenda for success and won't allow someone to bring her down. Some might mistake this attitude for arrogance or cockiness. Tia is neither. She is a straight-forward, strong-willed, independent-thinking young woman with a set of goals she intends to accomplish — to make sports history and to get a college education. She has no time for drugs, unwanted pregnancies, the trivialities of boyfriend troubles or bickering with girlfriends, and she certainly won't stand by and watch a friend throw her own life away. For example, if girls she knows become pregnant, Tia is clear: "I say, 'See ya, I'll stop in on my way back from the Olympics.'"

Having interviewed Tia and having watched her work out (she doubles our workouts), we're left to wonder if we could produce a "Tia pill" and pop it into the mouths of all young girls (not to mention our own mouths). At the very least, we wonder, why doesn't someone make a Tia doll?

As you have probably guessed, one of *our* favorite role models is Jackie Joyner-Kersee. We have always admired her for her athletic feats and the grace with which she wins and (rarely) loses. We have admired her because she was able to find her way out of a bad neighborhood by her own grit and determination and once she became a success, she returned to that very neighborhood, setting up a place for young people to get away from the streets. She found success and has created the opportunity for others to follow her. Like so many of our foremothers, Jackie Joyner-Kersee is a pioneer, paving a way for disadvantaged youngsters to find their way up. When we finally met this impressive woman, we were humbled. She speaks like she runs. She is elegant, focused, and concise.

She lectures to young people about "keeping your eyes on the prize." But too many young people have their priorities turned around, she says. The prize is not the gold medal; it is the hard work, doing the best you can do and fulfilling your dreams. In many ways, talking with Joyner-Kersee was similar to a discussion we had with ex-pro football and baseball player Bo Jackson. "To this day," Jackson says, "the most important thing I have is my education. It is the one thing no one can ever take away from me." Like Joyner-Kersee, Jackson tours the country, educating kids on health and exercise.

Joyner-Kersee pounds the point of "being the best you can be." Over and over she counsels young athletes to ask themselves, "How can *I* make this work? What can *I* do to be the best? How can *I* make this happen?" Believing in yourself, she says, is the key ingredient to success and happiness.

Joyner-Kersee is known to competitors around the globe, to reporters, and to anyone lucky enough to speak with her as one of the kindest, most gracious women in sports. Her prize, it turns out, is that she has captured our hearts.

The night we met her, a young all-American long distance runner was standing near Joyner-Kersee's waiting room, talking to us. We spoke quietly among ourselves, careful not to disturb Joyner-Kersee while she prepared her speech. Suddenly, we heard Joyner-Kersee speak up.

"You're a long distance runner?" came a voice. Shocked, the young runner looked to us for advice. *Should she answer? Should she peek her head around the corner?* Helpfully, we shrugged our shoulders at her.

Again, Joyner-Kersee spoke up, helping us in our awkwardness. "Wow, I really have respect for you. Shoot, I can't imagine doing that."

The runner grinned and stepped inside to swap track stories with Joyner-Kersee. Later, as Jackie Joyner-Kersee went on stage to do her thing, the young runner was still beaming. It was a night that meant everything to an aspiring Olympian. *Jackie Joyner-Kersee admires me!*

Just a couple months later, Joyner-Kersee would be an example of her own advice to "keep your eyes on the prize." During the Atlanta Games (her fourth and last Olympics), a pulled hamstring meant her withdrawal from the heptathlon, an event she had dominated for the past decade. Despite her injury, she participated in the long jump (her favorite event and another she had dominated for a decade). In obvious pain, she tried in vain to jump to her own standards while thousands cheered. She could not, and walked away with the bronze medal. Only later, in tears, did she say that this was her most moving Olympic experience. She realized that all those people didn't care if she won the gold or not. It hadn't mattered to them. It had only mattered that Joyner-Kersee showed them the heart, determination, and style of the champion she is. The prize was self-respect.

Throughout our interviews, as we have asked girls who their female role models are, we have been repeatedly struck by their uncertainties. Boys, on the other hand, seem to have no difficulty clearly identifying sports figures they admire. We learned that many male athletes credit their mothers. Indeed, we learned that boys can have positive, strong female role models as well, but it is a hard message to get out. For example, Reggie Miller of the Indiana Pacers *knew* that he would be a basketball star, and eventually an Olympian, after he watched his sister win a gold medal in the 1984 Olympic Games. Cheryl Miller, the first woman to dunk a basketball in regulation play (in high school), is his sister. "She made 105 points in one game," he smiles, "but who's counting?" Little brother Reggie, that's who.

But we need to do a better job of making women stronger, more recognizable role models for both sexes. We need to publicize the incredible feats women have accomplished — for both boys and girls. As corporations such as Nike and Reebok change their course of advertising, things are bound to improve. And already they have. Reebok and Nike both have put out strong messages about women and the benefits of sports — powerful images of the beauty of sport and sportswomen.

Representatives of HealthSouth, a company based in Dallas, Texas, tour the nation extolling the benefits of sport, promoting better and healthier lifestyles. With athletes such as Bo Jackson, Cory Everson, Troy Aikman, Kristy Yamaguchi, and Emmitt Smith (to name a few), HealthSouth educates children on the importance of physical education. During one such tour, we had the opportunity to meet Bo Jackson, golfer Tammi Green, basketball player Katie Smith, professional wrestler Lex Luger, and Minnesota Viking Robert Smith.

During the event, we were enchanted to watch as all the athletes doted over small children, encouraging them to race, jump, compete, and do the best they could. We watched Lex Luger flex his huge, tanned muscles and roar furiously at the kids, making them squeal with delight. Only 20 minutes earlier, we had met a very different man. While he calmly sat before us, quiet and serious, Luger explained to us the importance of role models. "Unfortunately, every time a celebrity rolls a car, is arrested for something, or is in a fight, the media picks up on that. It's the only thing you hear about. You don't hear about the good things some of these guys do."

Luger stresses the importance of trying to capture media attention for positive things, to let children and teens see the goodness and importance of positive role models. Like so many of the female athletes we spoke with, Lugar says that "giving back" is the key to being a good role model. A position he takes seriously.

And during the competition phase of the HealthSouth exercise, Luger was serious about trying to help his team, "The Purple Lightning," win. Robert Smith of the Minnesota Vikings was equally serious. It pained him to see one of his team players, a young girl about six years old, greatly outsized by her opponents. The object of the game was for each child to run to a large box and put on all the equipment that went with whatever sport flashed on an overhead screen. The little girl's sport was lacrosse.

She was off and running with the professional football player skulking behind her. Did he really think the hundreds of spectators wouldn't notice this large man looming over the small child? He must have, because when she could not gather all the equipment in her little arms, he scooped up the rest and hurried her back to the starting line, pretending to hide a helmet, a cleat, and a shin guard under his shirt. When his team won, they cheered and cheered together. We watched and saw that Smith had taken a special interest in the little girl and helped her out every chance he thought the several hundred people in attendance *weren't* looking his way!

He helped the little girl by letting her do her best, never stepping in until she couldn't hold any more. He showed her great affection, team spirit, and offered help when it was needed. But, most importantly, he made her feel included and important; he made her feel that she could do what the other kids were doing. Imagine if our kids had more of that kind of role model.

For Coleen Clark, there were no huge crowds, but then it was better that way. While running the treadmill at Accelerate Ohio, she got sick — as we have all done — and ran to the bathroom to throw up. She was too mortified to return to her workout. But to her surprise, when she peeked her head out, Ki-Jana Carter of the Cincinnati Bengals was waiting outside the locker room (having sent Clark's mother for some Gatorade).

"He told me he's thrown up, too," Clark smiled shyly.

Carter consoled Clark by saying that he had gotten sick from the hard workout (nevermind that he was clocked at 25 miles per hour), and assured her that she was doing a great job. Needless to say, Clark hopped right back on that treadmill!

As Luger points out, while many professional athletes are paid huge sums of money only to misbehave on and off the court, there are also many positive role models. Indeed, while no one is paying hockey player Karen Bye big bucks, and there are no impressive endorsements coming her way, she remains one of the finest role models today.

After her games, Bye makes it a habit to shake hands with fans. It is just part of the "giving back" attitude so many female athletes have. On one occasion, while she was shaking hands with fans, she noticed a little boy she had seen many times before. Every time she came near him, he sat perfectly still and stared at her, never daring to say a word. Bye would try to get him to talk, but he would only stare at her. (Although, according to his mother, he would talk excitedly about Bye the moment she was gone.)

Days later, Bye received a phone call from the little boy's mother. It seemed that the child idolized Bye, it was his birthday, and the mother wondered if Bye could come as a surprise. Bye obliged. Even as we heard this story, we wondered how many other athletes today would make themselves available for a child's birthday party.

When the little boy answered the door and saw Bye, he burst into tears, unable to speak. His hero had come to wish him a happy birthday. Bye said, "I didn't know what to do. I was hopping from foot to foot saying, 'Okay, let's play!'" The boy was so overwhelmed that he couldn't do anything.

"I haven't heard from him in about five years," she says good-naturedly. "I guess he grew up and thought, 'What am I doing wasting my time with that girl?'" While it is entirely likely that a boy did outgrow his hero-worship of a female hockey player, Bye continues to be a strong role model to everyone who knows her.

"I just recently received a letter from a 14-year-old girl from Seattle, Washington," Bye says. "She had attended our games in Vancouver back in April 1996." After commenting on how much she loved the games, the girl went on to write how much she would like to go to the 1998 Olympics with Bye. In the letter, the young girl offered her own idea to Bye about how this could be arranged. "Hey, I have a great idea," she wrote. "I will fly to

Japan with you, sit next to you on the plane and talk hockey, of course. Then, when we get there, we will rent a car (a Mazda 626 because you are number 6 and I am number 26). How does that sound?"

It sounded good enough for Bye to immediately write her back, answering all of her questions about women's hockey, and send her an autographed picture.

When we asked Nancy Woodhull (of the Media Studies Center) to name her two most influential female role models, she chose Billie Jean King and Betty Friedan.

"The first story that I covered (as a reporter) about a woman trying to change things for women was Billie Jean King in the early '70's," Woodhull told us. "King was trying to open the tennis circuit, get women playing in bigger tournaments, and give them access to bigger financial rewards. A couple of things happened for women journalists who followed and wrote about her. First, we were influenced and affected by her undaunted strategic approach to equality. Also, covering the story gave a lot of women journalists an opportunity because King was a page-one story, and editors believed only women could cover her story well. Covering Billie Jean was both a learning experience and a professional opportunity.

Nancy Woodhull

"Billie Jean King's professional rise was almost simultaneous with the reverberations from Betty Friedan's book *Feminine Mystique,* which were really being felt by women in a positive way. I wouldn't meet Betty until 25 years later when we started working together on how the press covered women. She had the same undaunted strategic and brave approach to dealing with women's issues that Billie Jean King did."

Like King and Friedan, Woodhull was a mighty storm, championing women's rights and educating the public. Labeled "feminists" (the dreaded "F" word), Friedan and Woodhull intimidated many over the years — Friedan with her exploration of "the woman problem" and co-foundership of the National Organization for Women (NOW), and Woodhull with her aggressive work as a journalist and women's advocate. As senior vice president of the Freedom Forum, executive director of the Media Studies Center, chair of the national advisory board for the National Women's Hall of Fame, vice-chair of the International Women's Media Foundation, and co-founder/co-chair of Men, Women and Media, Woodhull settled herself into the gutsy line of activist. To some, that's scary stuff.

But just as Woodhull was labeled with the "F" word, she taught us a thing or two about labeling. While we were busily creating the "Am I a Flower or a Storm?" chapter, in our minds anyone who was a cheerleader or drum majorette was certainly a flower. No storm would ever be a majorette, right? No one except Nancy Woodhull, lead majorette of the Matawan Regional High School. Woodhull was a majorette with style: she twirled with fire (while teachers stood by with fire extinguishers).

Woodhull's two passions were the Media Studies Center and her teenage daughter, Tennessee. Woodhull served as an incredibly influential role model, striving for her work at the Center to be "a catalyst for helping press be as good as it possibly can be and, two, that [my work there can] help be a catalyst for my daughter, whatever profession she goes into." Demonstrating her passion, Woodhull named her daughter after the sister of a strong-willed woman who was a suffragist and who actually ran for the presidency in 1870. Victoria Claflin Woodhull (no relation) and her sister, Tennessee, both believed in and spoke out for women's issues long before it became fashionable.

Nancy Woodhull continued that legacy — for her daughter, for all daughters — and did much to change perceptions about and acceptance of women in all forums.

There are thousands of unsung heroines around the country — women who, like Woodhull, are part of the storm. Women like Karen Powe.

Karen Powe is an unknown in the sports world, but we recognize her as our best friend and greatest fan. She has been our coach, manager, and cheerleader. What she cannot fully appreciate, since she herself is a quiet storm, is that she planted the seed of determination and persistence in us. Because she always told us we could be whatever we wanted to be, it had not occurred to us that our age or sex might be a problem in the world of bobsledding. Thank goodness for that. Like Julie Croteau, who was raised to believe that everyone is equal, we had difficulty understanding the lack of support for women joining the sport of bobsled. Our mother taught us not to back away from a fight for what is right. She taught us to go for the gold, and to go with gusto.

Sports history may not have included some of the pioneers named in this book and the thousands like them, but what an impact they have had: Greg Williams introducing mathercise to his kids, Tia Trent threatening to cut off her friend until she raised her grades, Allie Sizler being recruited by colleges at age 15, Danielle Lundy becoming a role model at age 11. These people send the real message to little girls: you do matter; you can make a difference.

Hilliard put it rather poignantly when she wrote, "Female athletic role models are touchable icons who live down the street. Their presence is a motivating force for girls, sending the message that playing sports is not only an acceptable thing to do but it's a status symbol."[2]

When we asked The Fabulous Sports Babe if she considers herself a role model, she replied, "Well, I do think I have an obligation not to be crawling into the back a police car at midnight with my coat pulled over my head." Even though she tells us that at home she's just "Nanci, who takes out the garbage," it is from home that she calls us to support this book for young girls, women, coaches, sports fans, and parents everywhere.

And as we wrote the book, we continued to be amazed by the women who lent themselves to our project. To pick up a ringing phone to hear, "Hi, this is Micki King," or "This is Christine Brennan. I just got your message. Am I too late?" The Fabulous Sports Babe gave us her home phone number in case we thought of other questions. We called Bonnie Blair at her sister's house. In fact, the interview began with her little nephew shouting into the telephone, "Buzz, buzz, the bee's gonna get you!" An embarrassed Blair only laughed and said, "Whew, I don't know what that was about. Anyway. . . ."

American Gladiator Eason (Sky) stayed up until midnight chatting on the phone with us. We sat at the dinner table with Karen Bye and Cammy Myler, swapping stories, and laughed with U.S. track treasure Wyomia Tyus. We actually forgot an important question for Mary Lou Retton because of her infectious, deep-belly laughs. We conspired with Janet Evans to write a funny autograph for a friend of ours. And Janet Evans and Mary Lou Retton are both as charming and truly nice as they appear to be in television interviews.

In so many instances, we snickered and giggled, swapped stories, exchanged telephone numbers, and listened intently to athletes who had once been total strangers as they all talked about something they believe in: the wonderment of sports, the confidence sports give girls, and the camaraderie of female athletes.

We had not one, but several sports agents comment on how lucky we were. "If you were trying to do this with a group of elite male athletes, it would have never happened. Every one of them would have wanted money."

Of all the athletes, the countless number of athletes we talked to, only one athlete's agent asked about money (and then dropped the subject). And it is clear in talking to sports agents like Debbie Zeily, Kristen Kaluga, and Robin Carr-Locke that they are all proud of their women clients, but not at all surprised.

In the meantime, we're working on the newest additions to the Barbie collection: the Tia, Allie, and Sameka dolls, guaranteed to speak up for what they believe in.

Cory (left), Jenna (lower left), Mary Lou (lower right), and Tia (bottom) are all examples of the female athlete as role model.

Chapter Twelve

Rrrrrocks for Sale!!!

> *Confidence and success —*
> *You need to know what it feels like and to know what you're going for.*
> — Nancy Woodhull

Becca Allred, only seven years old at the time, stood at the end of her street in Colstrip, Montana — a budding entrepreneur. Her sales stand complete, she readied herself for a day of business.

"Rrrrrrocks for sale!"

As her older brother, Robb, now likes to tease her, her slogan went something like this: "Rrrrocks for sale! Buy one, get one freeeee!" Nevermind that she stood only a few feet from the county rock pile. What makes this story special is that neighbors actually bought rocks from her. The very rocks they had littered all over their driveways, sidewalks, and streets.

It really didn't matter what she was selling. They were supporting *her*. They were supporting her initiative, her desire to succeed.

It is in that same spirit that Alex, having had a baby six months prior and still nursing, called her father to announce she was going to Lake Placid, New York, to try out for the U.S. bobsled team. Both of her parents were surprised but immediately supportive.

Alex was selling rocks and her parents were buying them up lock, stock, and barrel. They were also supportive (though a bit more concerned) when Michelle announced she also was trying out — eight months after neck surgery.

It is in that same spirit that Lyn St. James announced she was going to race cars and that Danielle Lundy said she was going to be an Olympic swimmer. It is in that same spirit that Rachael Myllymaki said at the age of nine she would be a professional rodeo rider and Sheryl Swoopes announced she would be a professional basketball player one day. Their parents all bought barrels full of rocks.

Rachael Myllymaki

Sometimes, the parents were the ones selling the rocks. For Bonnie Blair, her father was telling people she would win an Olympic medal when she was only twelve. Blair says she thought "he was nuts." Then, at the age of sixteen, she began to taste success and wanted more. Thus was born the greatest U.S. Winter Olympian. Karla Keck also thought her father was nuts when he said she could win the Junior Olympic trials. He also was right.

It seems fitting, then, as we near the end of this book, to give a special thanks to all the parents, coaches, and supporters of female athletics, for it is only because of them that our spirit survives. It is this very special group of people who hold things together when the appeal of the rock sale is lost. How many times has an athlete asked, "Why am I doing this?" to be answered by her coach, spouse, or parent? We opened the book with the chapter, "Why am I Doing This?," in which we looked at the range of emotions athletes experience, and named some of numerous rewards sports bring, including better health, fun, and companionship. There are times, though, when the athlete cannot find the answer to her question, or, at least, not an appropriate one. How many times has an athlete thought about bailing out only to be reeled back in by her mother, father, friend, and/or coach?

Take, for example, the Illinois State University women's soccer team. They had rapidly become the Bad News Bears of women's soccer. They were on a losing streak that was destroying team morale and personal relationships. The majority of the team were freshmen, and the team had suffered so many injuries that there were no substitutes. Several played injured.

As team member Beth Seidelmann put it, "This wasn't what we signed up for." To put it mildly, the season had become a huge disappointment. Coaches Nora Maguire, Scott Hollis, and Ashley Riggs went to work, introducing "Team Unity Games" into the workouts.

When asked about the unity games, the players lit up and told us about the games and their impact. In one example, a rope was tied between the soccer goal posts about six feet in the air, limbo-style. The object was for every player to make it over the rope without touching it. "It was hilarious," said team manager R.J. Rodriquez. "The first person just launched herself over the rope, landing flat out on the other side. The laughter broke down the barriers. It was really funny."

Then the team members made a human ladder, allowing each player to climb over the others. As they made it over, one by one, the team began to build again. The reason for playing soccer returned to the players.

The coaches also suspended a hula hoop from a rope and the players all had to jump through the hoop without touching it.

"We had to do it in less than 20 minutes," Heather Bowman laughed. Just remembering some of their stunts — leap frogging over people, dive bombing through the hoop — made the young athletes laugh again.

Then there was an exercise in which the women stood in a line about 20 feet away from assistant coach Riggs. They had to go from the line to Riggs without using their feet.

"If you can imagine human seals," laughed Riggs, "that's what they looked like. The whole team had to get to me without using their feet. They were all rolling over each other, like seal pups. It was hilarious."

But as Dr. Coleen Hacker, team psychologist for the U.S. women's soccer team, is quick to point out, "It's not all about laughter." It is about the messages these athletes take home: team unity, cooperation, trust, friendship, forgiveness, and loyalty.

Illinois player Kathie Cache concurred, "It taught us how to work with others, work as individuals to help the team."

"Communication is the key," Seidelmann piped in.

"Yeah, now I hear people on the field," said Kelly Bernard.

Even as we talked to them, there were little side glances they threw each other's ways, some inside story about someone, something that was really funny but that they were not sure they should share. We respect this. This is one of the treasures of team athletes and other groups who take risks together, depend on one another, and succeed or fail as a group. They have their own special club, and it is their coaches and leaders who help them pull through the hard times.

We actually conducted the soccer team interview in mid-flight on a trip from Nashville to Chicago. The Illinois State University women had just lost another game, but this time their spirits were high. "It was a close game, 1-0," Seidelmann said. "We cried after the game, you know, frustrated. But Nora told us, 'The important thing is you care about what you're doing. I can see it in your eyes. That's all that matters. You care. I'd take you guys any day.' That meant a lot to us."

The Illinois State University women's soccer team has not been alone. The U.S. women's bobsled team has had its share of problems as well. As with any sport, external problems can eat away at a team. If you have a rickety ship, you need to have a tight crew. In the beginning stages of the women's program, we were anything but. Internal fighting, petty jealousy, and name calling were destroying the 1994 U.S. Nationals. In reality, there were only two athletes (both gone now) causing the problems, but often times that's all it takes. Women were taking sides, not communicating. Enough was enough. Coach Steve Maiorca slapped a note on our bulletin board:

Gymnasium: 4:00 Mandatory!

As the women trudged into the gymnasium, snarling at each other, Maiorca stood defiantly at the end of the volleyball court with a ball tucked under his arm. Using the finger-pointing method, he divided the women into teams and clapped his hands. The game was underway. For two hours, the U.S. women's bobsled team slam-dunked, dove, slid, pummeled, taunted, and teased. What started out as pure aggression ended with much laughter and a new-found team spirit.

When Maiorca finally waved his hand at us to get out, we all ran to the physical therapy room and dunked our bruised and throbbing forearms into the ice bath.

"Ahhhh," sighed the chorus of women as we crowded around the pool. That was it; for that season, that was all it took for most of us. The others left the team.

In whatever capacity, coaches have encouraged and carried so many of the athletes with whom we talked. In fact, it was during a yellow belt examination at the Westerville Tae Kwon Do martial arts school that head instructor David Perdue exemplified the oneness that coaches often feel with their athletes. Together, Perdue and a special student had trained and struggled. Perdue knew that his student *knew* his material. But before dozens of on-lookers, little James Budd forgot.

After the physical test comes the verbal test. The question was, "What is the name of the form you just did?"

"Chung Ji," came the answer.

"And what does it mean?"

We all watched helplessly as James' little 40-pound body squirmed. Perdue's dark and intense eyes narrowed, boring holes into the little person. Flanked by four black belt instructors, Perdue looked intimidating.

Silence.

Perdue leaned forward in his chair, studying the boy for a moment. He then looked up to the ceiling and, then, down to the ground. He was signaling the answer: "Heaven and Earth."

Nothing. James didn't catch on.

Perdue tried again. With exaggeration, he strained his eyes up toward the ceiling for several seconds and, then, while parents and students chuckled, down to the ground.

"Um," little Budd struggled.

Yes, yes. Perdue could see he almost had it. Again, he did a Superman gaze at the ceiling, and back down to the floor.

"Ceiling and Earth, Sir!" the boy proudly said.

The room erupted in laughter and Perdue nodded. Close enough.

Like Minnesota Vikings player Robert Smith, Perdue has a keen sense of what is important. It is not that little girls or boys complete tasks all alone, but that they are willing to try, and learn that with a little encouragement they can do anything!

After everything we have discussed in this book, after all the stories, the sagas and drama, in the end, life is about encouragement, isn't it? From the beginning of life, two or more people cheer on a laboring mother to "Push, Push," and when the healthy baby arrives, we cheer and cheer. We give congratulations and cigars, put up signs, and send out announcements.

From there, life gets a lot harder. That is why sports are so wonderful. Sports afford the opportunity for people to cheer you. Rarely will you be cheered simply for entering a grocery store, eating a McDonald's burger, or surfing television channels. Sports allow you to meet, befriend, work with, sometimes travel with, talk to, giggle with and, best of all, play with supportive people.

Oregon City High School's girls' basketball team get just that kind of support from their town, and repay it in kind. The undefeated Pioneers (nationally ranked number one) raise their own travel funds by selling t-shirts and autographed posters. "This team," says state lobbyist Ralph Groener, "is what people talk about at the barbershop, at the grocery store, at the paper mill. Girl's basketball has kept us together."[1]

Indeed, sports can bring together the most unlikely alliances. Bobsledding has been so demanding, exhausting, sometimes cruel that we have stuck together, forming a bond that will carry through our entire lives. Isn't that incredible? Isn't it something to think that through sport people from all over the globe can form such strong bonds and reap such wonderful benefits?

A motivational speaker we heard recently pointed out again and again how wonderful our world would be if we all watched our words; held back the negative; and focused on positive statements, thinking, and actions. At that, he asked half the room to stand and face the sitting half. On the count of three, the standers were to yell, holler, cheer as never before — so loudly that everyone else in the building would wonder, "Are they having an Amway meeting?"

The sitting half was then instructed to stand and take bows, turn and high-five the people around, as though they'd just done a great thing. Then, that half of the room returned the cheers while the other half bowed, high-fived, and giggled.

It was a great moment. Most of the people in the room were not athletes, but parents, grandparents, and sports fans. They themselves might not have ever heard cheers like that before. It was a wonderful, warm feeling that demonstrated the feeling of giving and getting support.

That's what this chapter (the book, really) is about. It is about standing ovations, supporting other people, being a great teammate, and believing in what you are selling — whether it's rocks or your future as an Olympic speedskater or swimmer, or as a professional rodeo rider!

As Denise Perdue says, "I guess I got my black belt because I was determined to show everyone that I could do it. I had worked very hard to achieve that goal. I think that it's the dedication more than skill that enables anyone to achieve their goals."

While we have demonstrated time and time again how athletes themselves become great cheerleaders (case in point — how many were willing to talk to us), it is the families who have carried most of the athletes.

It was David Perdue who encouraged Denise Perdue to take up the martial arts when she tired of aerobics. A whole new world has been opened to her. In fact, we see many husband and wife teams in the sports world. Jackie Joyner-Kersee is married to husband/coach Bob Kersee. Gwen Torrence is married to husband/coach Manley Waller. Sandra Farmer-Patrick, Michelle Rohl, Valerie Still all married fellow athletes (all in the same sport). In fact, Still's husband Robert Locke agreed to stay home with their son Aaron while Still plays professional ball. It is a role reversal that has been difficult for Locke to adjust to, but — because of his tremendous love and support for Still — Locke is holding down the fort.

Bonnie Blair is convinced that her family gave her the winning edge. They became known as the Blair Bunch during the Olympics, and their support for her made them known and admired worldwide. During the Calgary Games, there were 25 family members present. At the Albertville Games, 45 family members came. In Lillihammer, there were 60; and for her final speedskating competition during the 1995 World championships in Milwaukee, Blair had 300 family members present. How could she possibly lose? She says, "There wasn't any pressure because they were there for me all along." Even if she had lost, she still would have won.

When we begin to believe that we are in fact selling diamonds rather than rocks, the mind-set of our ESPN executive *will* change. The Old Guard *will* fall. From following the Women's Sports Foundation guidelines for setting up grants for local athletes to ensuring better health care for women and girls, we have to make sure things change. Then, as Valerie Still suggests, there might come a time when corporations and sports franchises write child care into athletes' contracts.

For Clair Rheul, mother of U.S. diver Becky Rheul, it wasn't enough that she had taught her daughter about sportsmanship; it wasn't enough that Becky was a champion (both in body and soul); Clair Rheul wanted more for *all* young athletes. Too many times she had seen the pressures of a coach or parent destroy the purpose of sport and the drive of a young child.

For this reason, she created a handbook outlining guidelines for parents, coaches, and athletes at Villa Madonna Academy, where Becky dives. Clair Rheul sees to it that everyone at Villa Madonna — athletes, parents, coaches — gets a crash course in sportsmanship.

The handbook reads as follows:

Parent's Code

> Parents embark on a unique journey as they allow their child to enter the world of sports. This world provides the student with an arena for exercise, competition, and learning about life. It provides the parent with the opportunity to teach, communicate, and build character and self-esteem in their child. While winning a game can be exciting and inspirational, Villa Madonna parents are expected to help teach students that winning does not define the importance or worth of either the school, the team or the individual player.

Villa Madonna's Sports Pledge for Parents

I will always be supportive.

I will never coach from the sideline.

I will never yell negative remarks at players, other teams, or referees.

I will never seek to humiliate or embarrass.

I will never reserve acceptance and praise for athletic performance.

I will help the athlete to set realistic goals.

I will provide a shoulder to cry on when needed and a "high five" when earned.

I will teach sports etiquette and good sportsmanship.

I will educate the athlete regarding team loyalty and responsibility.

I will help the athlete to communicate with the coaching staff in a positive way.

I will support the coaching staff.

I will relinquish the responsibility for my child's participation in the sport to the coach for the period of the contest.

I will follow the line of communication to resolve problems as set forth in the *Rules and Guidelines of Coaches*.

I will always cheer the athlete and the team.

Coach's Code

In many respects, a coach's responsibility is similar to that of a teacher, but in some ways, it is even more challenging because he or she is attempting to modify the behavior of both mind and body. The school and parents are depending on the coach for the welfare of the student as well as for developing proper attitudes and physical skills. The coach often is in the position during pressurized and competitive situations to demonstrate moral leadership. The coach is often in the unique position of being liked, trusted and respected in an informal atmosphere. In effect, a coach can bridge the gap between home and school life. At Villa Madonna, our coaches are expected to accept responsibility as well as the rewards of the furthering development of a student.

We have adopted the "National Youth Sports Coaches Association Code of Ethics Pledge" which states:

I will place the emotional and physical well-being of my players ahead of any personal desire to win.

I will remember to treat each player as an individual, remembering the large spread of emotional and physical development for the same age group.

I will do my very best to provide a safe situation for my players.

I promise to review and practice the necessary first-aid principles needed to treat injuries of my players.

I will do my best to organize practices that are fun and challenging for all my players.

I will lead, by example, in demonstrating fair play and sportsmanship to all my players.

I will ensure that I am knowledgeable in the rules of each sport that I coach and that I will teach these rules to my players.

I will use those coaching techniques appropriate for each of the skills that I teach.

I will remember that I am a youth coach, and that the game is for the children and not the adults.

Athlete's Code

Athletes who participate in organized school sports have a tremendous opportunity for growth. Athletes develop their strength, coordination, endurance, and specific skills related to the sport they play. But athletes would be missing the greatest gifts sports have to offer if they limited themselves to physical prowess. Athletes who have gained the most from sports have allowed their minds and spirits, as well as their bodies, to grow as they experience the wins and losses of organized sports. Those who have challenged themselves to be the best they can be, not just in the game, but during practice as well, will develop characteristics they will use throughout their life. Sports, if allowed, will teach athletes about never giving up, about taking pride in all they do, about feeling joy or empathy for others, about making friends, but mostly sports will teach athletes to believe in themselves.

Villa Madonna's Sports Pledge for Athletes

I will always be a good sport, whether winning or losing.

I will always show respect for all players, coaches, and officials.

I will never use obscene language or gestures.

I will support my team in a positive way, whether playing or on the sidelines.

I will not argue with my coach or officials.

I will give my best effort and attention at practice and during games.

I will play fair and follow the rules of the game.

I will remember that sport is a game and I will have fun playing.

•••

Thank you, Clair Rheul. These are lessons all athletes and supporters of athletes should learn and follow. We are all connected to one another, and should support one another.

In fact, we the authors broke a lifelong record of *never* watching a golf tournament to watch Tiger Woods make history. And when Woods did the unthinkable and became the youngest man and first African-American to win the Master's by the largest margin in its history, he shared his accomplishment with Lee Elder (the first black to ever play in a Master's) and all the golfers of color who preceded him, who made his victory possible. Yeah, sure, this is a book about women and sports, but we as women understand that sports (like life) should transcend gender and race.

Before our flight from Nashville to Chicago landed, the Illinois State University women's soccer team coerced the flight attendants into thanking their coaching staff over the loudspeaker so the entire plane could applaud the efforts of the coaches. It didn't matter that they had lost the game. While we all clapped, the coaches and trainers looked sheepish and very pleased. It is the little thanks and the little encouragement we all get that help us carry on and believe.

It's a different spin, of course, but we have our own set of guidelines we think would be nice if people could follow — not just in sports, but in life. The following story was shared with us by Elda Huling:

A Lesson in Cooperation from Geese

Next fall when you see geese heading south for the winter, flying along in a "V" formation, you might be interested in knowing what science has discovered about why they fly that way. As each bird flaps its wings, it creates an uplift for the bird immediately following. By flying in a "V" formation, the whole flock adds at least 71 percent greater flying range than if each bird flew on its own.

Whenever a goose falls out of formation, it suddenly feels the drag and resistance of trying to go it alone, and quickly gets into formation to take advantage of the lifting power of the bird immediately in front. When the lead goose gets tired, he rotates back in the "V" and another goose flies point. The geese honk from behind to encourage those up front to keep up their speed. Finally, when a goose gets sick, or is wounded by a gun shot and falls out, two geese fall out of formation and follow him down to help or protect him. They stay with him until he is either able to fly again or until he is dead, and they then launch out on their own or with another formation to catch up with the group.

People who share a common direction and sense of community also can get where they are going more quickly and easily because they are traveling on the uplift of one another.

If geese can figure this out, why can't we?!

Sonja Tate holds Katie Allred while being interviewed for this book — where else but women's sports?

Chapter Thirteen

The Pot of Gold

"You'll never be a professional, so just enjoy the game. Don't put up with the b.s., but only fight the battles you can win." This was a sincere statement made by the ESPN executive, meant to encourage little girls to just enjoy games but to not take them too seriously. The executive hastened to add that the most important lesson in sports is personal growth, but it hadn't occurred to him that once he told his daughter she could never excel to the same level as boys, there was no room for personal growth; she was already in shut-down mode.

> *"And she found herself glowing inside.*
> *Somebody wanted her to play.*
> *Somebody thought it natural for her to play."*
>
> — Zora Neale Hurston, ***Their Eyes Were Watching God***

Who knows how many athletes we lose when girls are discouraged from taking sports seriously? How many business executives, political leaders, or community leaders? Sports teach the basic rules of group organization and interaction, rules that we need to teach our girls, as well as our boys, if we want a truly equitable society.

As Lopiano of the Women's Sports Foundation says: "Sport has been one of the most important socio-cultural learning experiences for boys and men for many years. . . . Sport is where boys have traditionally learned about teamwork, goal-setting, the pursuit of excellence in performance, and other achievement-oriented behaviors — critical skills for success in the workplace. In this economic environment, the quality of our children's lives will be dependent on two-income families. So both parents should have the advantage of experience in sport."[1]

Who knows how many happy, well-adjusted teenage girls and young women we lose by discouraging them from sports, by preventing them from gaining the self-confidence and pride that accompany sports? How many girls do we limit?

Lydia Stephans, vice president of ABC Sports and silver medalist in speedskating, sees sports as a "wonderful way to test yourself both physically and mentally." She contends that sports allow children an avenue to act out dreams and become whatever they want. Sports are not — ideally, anyway — about multimillion deals, fame and fortune, but about dreams and personal goals. They are about reaching the rainbow.

During the 1972 Olympics, Stephans stayed up late to watch the Games against the orders of her parents. She was especially interested in two Olympic hopefuls from her hometown of Northbrook, Illinois — Diane Holum and Anne Henning. "Until that point I wanted to be Janis Joplin," Stephans says. "You know how 12-year-olds are: one week it was Janis, and the next I wanted to be a speedskater."

As Stephans watched her heroines win gold, she realized if they could do it, so could she. Identifying with the two athletes from her hometown spurred her own dreams. Although her parents had never actually told her she *couldn't* be Janis Joplin, they were thrilled (perhaps relieved) at the idea of her becoming an athlete. From a rock-and-roll-lover to the vice president of ABC Sports, Stephans serves to remind us that the female athlete is confined only by the boundaries she allows someone to set for her.

"The best advice I ever got," Stephans says, "was from the first coach I ever had. He was the father of one of the other skaters. He didn't care if we won any races; all he ever cared was that we got up and finished the race if we fell." She fell a lot, she says, but the lesson was clear. "When you start something, see it through."

Learning to play with and work with others, testing oneself and learning to survive failure, working for and achieving personal goals — these are the most important lessons any female athlete or non-athlete must learn. When Julie Croteau sued her high school, it had never occurred to her that her coach would lie on the stand. Her parents had instilled in her a sense of fair play, so her coach's behavior was a blow to her. But did she really lose? Many would say she did, but the day she decided to carry out her dream of being a baseball player, she won. And by fighting that battle, she won for every little girl who can now dream about being a baseball player.

Our own mother, the source of our determination and power, gave us the greatest gift: she taught us that disappointment does not equal failure! Every time a girl or woman takes to the pitcher's mound, scales a mountainside, dives into a pool, fields a pop-fly, or clears the net with the perfect "swoosh," all of womankind has been triumphant. Believing that they can achieve anything is a confidence taught to boys, but not so often to girls.

That confidence is multi-faceted; it comes from many sources, and it shapes so many aspects of our personalities. We must continue to encourage girls into sports, teaching them competitive skills and confidence in school and business. And we must take responsibility for the images of femininity and female attractiveness we are sending to our children, so that we can teach them confidence in their own self-images and self-worths. The reality is our young girls will always be confronted by images of sexy women. It is okay for us to appreciate beauty, but we shouldn't feel the need to emulate those images in order to be worthwhile. We must give girls the chance to grow up into confident, healthy women, secure in who they are.

Sports are so important for girls and women because they teach us to be proud, not only of our abilities, but of our bodies. We don't get the benefits of oil and shaded lighting in the real world. We can't spend all of our time posing in front of mirrors and cameras. If we try or if we spend our lives comparing ourselves to others, we will be miserable. The reality is we get what we're born with. Through sports, we can spend months and years making our bodies — and minds — healthy and strong. That is enough.

When girls can acquire that confidence, there is no stopping them. Look at Lydia Stephans. Look at Julie Croteau.

While Stephans may have wanted to be Janis Joplin, Alice Coachman wanted to be Shirley Temple. Instead, she settled for the gold medal in high jumping during the 1948 Olympics, after having held the U.S. high jump title for 10 years. No other U.S. Olympic gold medalist, man or woman, has achieved 10 national championships. Coachman was also the first woman to bring home a gold medal in U.S. track and field and the first black women ever to win an Olympic gold medal. Despite the racism and poverty her family endured during the Depression, Coachman received a college education, traveled abroad, spoke with royalty, and saw things most people never got to see. As Coachman put it, "I was poor and black, and I had no track shoes. But my eyes were on the prize."[2] And like Jackie Joyner-Kersee, Coachman's prize was more than a gold medal. It was self-esteem, pride, accomplishment.

This is what we want girls to learn, to emulate. Alex's babies, Kerri and Katie — three and one years old, respectively — were with us on so many of our interviews. While we interviewed athletes at Accelerate Ohio, the girls were often with us, watching people run the treadmill. We watched as Katie carried an 11-pound medicine ball around, barely able to hold it, and played with baseballs, and we hoped a seed had been planted — that it was perfectly normal for her to push herself physically and for Mommy to talk sports.

Katie Allred

Our mother was not terribly athletic, but she participated in some way with us all our lives — as coach, cheerleader, team manager. But by the tender ages of 10 and 12, we had learned that it was not a good idea for Mom to actually *play* complex games, like "Duck, Duck, Goose." So one day when we were at soccer practice, waiting with the rest of our soccer team for the head coach, we both cringed when someone suggested that we play a tag game. We held our breaths when someone tapped Mom. She started off well, hopping to her feet, chasing the player around the circle. About ten steps into it, however, she — and we're still not sure how she managed this — fell and broke her big toe. The game was promptly ended and Mom spent the rest of practice with her foot elevated on the cooler.

We still laugh about how silly she looked and what a good sport she was, and we hope Kerri and Katie will have similar stories to tell about their times with us (but about more graceful events, we hope). Our point is that athletically-inclined or not, it is vital for parents to support their children in athletics. The reason so many successful athletes, in turn, give time to events for kids is because they know how important it is to have someone believe in you — so you can believe in yourself. Whether your mother is an American Gladiator, like Sky, or the best cheerleader in the whole world, like Karen Powe, knowing that she supports you and believes in you is half of the success right there!

Karen Bye's father has been her biggest supporter from the very beginning. In fact, he was responsible for starting Bye's hockey career. One evening when Bye was just seven years old, her older brother was sick and could not attend his hockey practice. Bye's father asked her if she wanted to put on her brother's equipment, go to his practice, and see if she could fool anyone into thinking she was her brother. "Whenever any of the guys would come up and talk to me (thinking that I was Chris), I would turn my head away and ignore them. After a while, they figured out it was me, but I had so much fun at that practice that my dad signed me up for hockey the following year." How great that Bye's father never even thought to limit her. Look at her now.

Today's female athlete can follow in the wake of the past hurricanes. Althea Gibson became the first black athlete, man or woman, to play at Wimbledon. Danielle Lundy hopes to be the first African-American swimmer to win gold. Wilma Rudolph, who wore leg braces for most of her childhood, was a three-time gold medalist in track and field. Julie Croteau was the first woman to play men's collegiate and professional baseball. Despite overwhelming odds against them, these women blew or are blowing down whole forests of resistance and oppression with their determination, allowing new hope to flourish.

As for the U.S. women's bobsled team, we plan to be our own storm on the way to gaining our goals and, we hope, to providing more opportunities for the athletes who follow us. We hope the names of the U.S. women bobsledders will soon be known to winter sports fans everywhere. The drivers: Jill Bakken, with her coloring books; Michelle Powe, who fought many of the initial battles for the team's rights to travel and compete — to exist; Chrissy Spiezio, whose silliness keeps us all smiling; and Jean Racine, who at 18 is the new "kid" on the block. The brakewomen: Liz Parr-Smestad and Alex Powe-Allred, the two mothers — Liz also acting as team mother and standing as a symbol of physical determination, and Alex remaining the cornerstone for the team, providing information and playing peacemaker (although she reverts back to her childhood whenever she sees Chrissy); Elena Primerano, who cross-trains between bobsledding and cycling; Meg Henderson, who is trying to balance bobsledding and medical school; Sue Blazejewski, who trained for the team trials by pulling a tourist rickshaw in Miami; and powerlifter Krista Ford whose tremendous power and sportsmanship bring credibility to the team.

The message we — as members of the U.S. women's bobsled team — want to send to you is the same as that of all the athletes who graced the pages of this book with their spirit. It doesn't matter who you are, what your goals are, or what you want in life, only that you give life your best shot! As Rachael Myllymaki puts it, "The sky's the limit. But the only way you're going to achieve your dreams is to go for it. No one is going to give it to you." So, we say simply, *go for it.* Dare to dream and reap the rewards, and in the words of the great Dr. Seuss:

> *"You'll be on your way up! You'll be seeing great sights!*
> *You'll join the high fliers who soar to high heights.*
> *You won't lag behind, because you'll have the speed.*
> *You'll pass the whole gang and you'll soon take the lead.*
> *Wherever you fly, you'll be the best of the best.*
> *Wherever you go, you will top all the rest!"*

Good luck in whatever you do!

"THROUGH AND DOWN"

Notes

Introduction

1. Richard Zoglin, "The Girls of Summer," *Time* (August 12, 1996, 50.)
2. Claudia Glenn Dowling, "The Other Dream Team," *TV Guide* (July 27-August 2, 1996), 17.
3. Mary Pipher, *Reviving Ophelia: Saving the Selves of Adolescent Girls* (NY: Ballantine Books, 1994), 27.
4. Bob Hunter, "Dream Team Couldn't Hold Candle To Women," *The Columbus Dispatch* (August 9, 1996), 1Sports.
5. Cecil Harris, "Women Not Equal Yet At Olympics," The *Standard Star* (Westchester County, NY) (July 20, 1996).
6. Gene Yasuda, "Olympics, pro teams give boost to girls' athletics," *The Columbus Dispatch* (August 9, 1996, 3F).

Chapter One: Why am I Doing This?

1. Wendy Hilliard, "Our Own Worst Enemy?," *Women's Sports & Fitness* (September 1996), 38.
2. Mary Pipher, *Reviving Ophelia*, 22.
3. Radu Teodorescu, with Maura Rhodes, *Radu's Simply Fit* (NY: Cader Books, 1996), 3.
4. "Oprah Buff," *People* (September 9, 1996), 81.
5. Nancy Lieberman-Cline, "Communities should support, honor girls in sports," *The Dallas Morning News* (July 11, 1996), 2B.
6. "At 82, she says long walks home take the workday's cares away," *The Columbus Dispatch* (July 11, 1996), 3B.
7. Jane Gottesman, "Your Grandma Wears Hiking Boots," *Women's Sports & Fitness* (May 1997), 51.
8. Alexander Wolff, "Power Grab," *Sports Illustrated* (August 12, 1996), 59.
9. Monica Seles with Nancy Ann Richardson, "Advantage: Courage," *Reader's Digest* (September 1996), 130-31.

Chapter Two: Am I a Flower or a Storm?

1. Wayne Westcott, Joyce Tolken and Brian Wessner, "School-Based Conditioning Programs for Physically Unfit Children," *Strength and Conditioning* (April 1995), 5.
2. Gabrielle Reece and Karen Karbo, *Big Girl in the Middle* (NY: Crown Publishing, 1997), 83.
3. Wendy Hilliard, "The Trickle-Down Effect," *Women's Sports & Fitness* (October 1996), 55.
4. Hillary Rodham Clinton, "It Takes a Village," *Working Woman* (May 1996), 30.

Chapter Three: The Goddess Within

1. "Mission Impossible: Deluged by images from TV, movies, and magazines, teenage girls do battle with an increasingly unrealistic standard of beauty — and pay a price," *People* (June 3, 1996), 66-68.
2. "Thumps/ You've Got to Be Kidding," *New Woman* (April 1996), 156.
3. Rick Riley, "Behold the Rising Star of the GDR," *Sports Illustrated* (Jan. 20, 1986), 38.
4. Eric Davis, "Some Thoughts on Local Girls' Cage Season," *The Marion Star* (March 31, 1996), 3B.
5. Eric Davis, "Sorry, Lady Vikes; You Were Great, Too," *The Marion Star* (April 7, 1996), 3B.
6. "Heroine Worship: Most Valuable Player," *The New York Times Magazine* (November 24, 1996), 62.
7. Richard Hoffer, "Gritty Woman," *Sports Illustrated* (April 15, 1996), 58.
8. Eileen Glanton, "Mighty 'Xena' heroically battles for justice, ratings in syndication," *The Columbus Dispatch* (October 27-November 2, 1996), Teleview Plus 26.
9. Chuck Arnold, "Chatter," *People* (March 10, 1997), 128.

Chapter Four: The Athlete Within

1. "Naked Power, Amazing Grace," *Life* (July 1996), 57.
2. Mary Ellen Clark "Dizzying Heights," *Guideposts* (January 1997), 4-7.
3. Christine Vaccaro Lawson, "Mary Ellen Clark's New Platform," *Women's Sports & Fitness* (June 1997), 65.

4. Kathrine V. Switzer, "From 'K.V. Switzer' to Girl to Woman in the Span of 4 1/2 Hours," *The New York Times* (April 13, 1996). p9, sec 8.

5. Alan Baldwin, "Quirot Ran to Stay Alive," *Reuters* (July 29, 1996).

6. Bonnie Blair, *A Winning Edge* (Dallas: Taylor Publishing, 1996).

Chapter Five: Are You a Mother or an Athlete?

1. Anna Seaton Huntington, "Superstar. . . You Got A Problem With That?," *Women's Sports & Fitness* (November/December 1996), 51.

Chapter Six: Journeymen

1. "Lisa Fernandez," *Women's Sports & Fitness* (October 1996), WSF Special Section.

2. Merrell Noden, "Catching Up With Runner Mary Decker Slaney," *Sports Illustrated* (Feb. 17, 1997), 4.

Chapter Seven: Bumper Stickers In Time Square

1. "Thumps/You've Got To Be Kidding," *New Woman* (April 1996), 156.

2. Martina Navratilova, "Game, Set, Set, Set, Match," *New York Times* (August 26, 1996), 15.

3. "Heroine Worship: Most Valuable Player," *The New York Times Magazine* (November 24, 1996), 62.

4. Donna Lopiano, "Don't Touch That Dial," *Women's Sports & Fitness* (July/August 1996), 42.

5. Linda Robertson, "Shattering the Glass Ceiling," *Association for Women in Sports Media* (Spring 1995), 2.

Chapter Eight: Toting the Chain

1. Donna Lopiano, "The Importance of Sports Opportunities for Our Daughters," *Women's Sports Foundation*, 6-7.
2. Benita Fitzgerald Mosley, "Entitled by Title IX," *Women's Sports & Fitness* (June 1997), 28.
3. Sarah Odell, "The Girls Against The Boys," *Elle* (Nov. 1996), 196-201.
4. Anna Seaton-Huntington, "The America's Cup Race Is Over. What Did Women Prove?," *Glamour* (July 1995).

Chapter Nine: Entering The Boys' Club

1. Jill Lieber, "A Road Less Taken," *Sports Illustrated* (May 3, 1993), 53-55.
2. Julie Tache, "Gender questions are part of answers," *The Association for Women in Sports Media* (Spring 1995), 4.
3. Lisa Winston, "Infiltrating the male domain," *AWSM* (Spring 1995), 1.

Chapter Ten: You've Come a Long Way, Baby

1. Dot Richardson, "Sex, Lies and Softball," *Sports Illustrated Women/Sport* (Spring 1997), 42-44.

Chapter Eleven: The Quietest of Storms

1. "A League of Her Own," *Sports Illustrated Women/Sport* (Spring 1997), 26.

2. Wendy Hilliard, "The Trickle-Down Effect," *Women's Sports & Fitness* (October 1996), 55.

Chapter Twelve: Rrrrrocks for Sale!!!

1. "Dateline: Oh! Pioneers! These Girls Next Door Are the Ultimate High School Heroes," *Sports Illustrated* (January 24, 1997), 28.

Chapter Thirteen: Pot of Gold

1. Donna Lopiano, "The Importance of Sport Opportunities for Our Daughters," *Women's Sports Foundation*, 1.
2. Alice Coachman, "An Olympian Looks Back." *Women's Sports &Fitness* (July/August 1996), 114.

Photography Credits:

pages viii, 25, 227: photos provided by the family of Nancy Woodhull.
pages 7, 20 : photos provided by Julie Croteau.
pages 14, 96, 109, 132, 158, 184, 216, 348, 353: photos from the collection of Alex Powe-Allred.
page 17: photo provided by Roger Lundy, Jr.
pages 35, 232: photos provided by Jenna Brader.
pages 38, 232: photos provided by Tia Trent.
page 41: photos provided by the Winter Sports Foundation.
page 48: photo provided by Christine Brennan.
page 59: photo provided by Wendy Hilliard.
pages 64, 232: photos provided by Mary Lou Retton.
pages 71, 232: photos provided by Cory Everson.
pages 80, 158, 178, 263: photos provided by Karen Powe.
page 85: photo © 1997 John Todd
page 127: photo provided by Bonnie Blair.
page 144: photos provided by Micki King.
page 168: photos provided by Anita DeFrantz.
page 172: photo provided by Donna Lopiano.
page 201: photos provided by Lyn St. James Racing LLC
pages 202, 234: photos provided by Rachael Myllymaki.

About the Authors

Alexandra Powe-Allred is a member of the U.S. Women's Bobsledding team, a full-time author and the mother of two.

Michelle Powe is also a member of the U.S. Women's Bobsledding team and a college English teacher away from the track.